Strictly Come Dancing

Strictly Come Dancing

Rupert Smith

Dance consultant: Len Goodman

BBC
BOOKS

First published in 2005
This revised and updated edition published in 2006 by
BBC Books, an imprint of Ebury Publishing

3 5 7 9 10 8 6 4 2

Ebury Publishing is a division of the Random House Group Ltd.

The Random House Group Ltd Reg. No. 954009

Addresses for companies within the Random House Group Ltd can
be found at www.randomhouse.co.uk

A CIP catalogue record for this book is available from the
British Library.

The Random House Group Ltd makes every effort to ensure that the
papers used in our books are made from trees that have been legally
sourced from well-managed and credibly certified forests. Our paper
procurement policy can be found at www.randomhouse.co.uk

Commissioning Editors: Nicky Ross and Stuart Cooper
Project Editor: Laura Nickoll
Designer: Bobby Birchall
Production Controller: Kenneth McKay
Step-by-step dance photography: GMK

Set in Minion and Frutiger
Printed and bound in Great Britain by CPI Bath
Colour separations by Dot Gradations Ltd, UK

ISBN 978 0 563 49379 2 (from Jan 2007)
ISBN 0 563 49379 8

Picture credits: pp. 43, 47 (top), 130, 134, 138, 142, 146, 150, 154, 158,
162, 166 BBC Photographic Archives; p. 47 (bottom) © ABC
Photographic Archives (Evander Holyfield); p. 170 © Patrik
Giardino/CORBIS; p. 174 © Jose Luis Pelaez, Inc./CORBIS;
p. 178 © Robbie Jack/CORBIS
All other photographs © BBC and © BBC Worldwide Ltd

BBC Books would like to thank photographers Gregory King,
David Venni, Ian Derry and Mark Whitfield.

Contents

Foreword

The third series of *Strictly Come Dancing* really took the show into a different league. It was a great mix of celebrities, and the competition seemed to be even more intense and exciting than ever before. The whole nation seems to have taken the show to its heart in a way that we could never have believed would happen. If you look at *Strictly Come Dancing* as an idea on paper, it shouldn't work – but it does. Everywhere I go, in the supermarket or the airport, people are always coming up to me and asking 'When

is *Strictly Come Dancing* coming back?'. You can't ask for more than that.

At the beginning of every show, I always say 'Now let's meet the stars' – the celebrities and the dancers – and I mean it. They're what it's all about. We can relate to all of them because they're already familiar faces, and we can go through all the highs and lows with them. I'm always amazed by their bravery; they're doing things live on television in front of millions of people that are way outside of their comfort zone. That takes guts, and I couldn't admire them more.

Every series gets a bit longer. This series is 12 weeks and we've got 14 competing pairs. It'll be a lot more work, but we can cope – and I think the competition will be even more exciting. If you add to that the music, the dancing, the fashion, the comedy with the judges, you have a show that appeals to absolutely everyone. Children especially seem to love it; it's something that they can't get from their Playstations! Ever since I first went on television in 1958, I've done shows that cater for children, and now with *Strictly Come Dancing* I've got them all over again. Another generation is growing up with me, and I couldn't be happier.

BRUCE FORSYTH

The 2005 series of *Strictly Come Dancing* was bigger and better than ever before. It reached a wider audience, it beat off all the competition and became the biggest entertainment show of the season. It really seemed to go to another level: everyone I met in the street or the supermarket wanted to talk to me about it. I felt like I was part of the most exciting thing that was happening. A lot of that was to do with Darren Gough; he captured people's imagination in a way nobody else has done before. And he got a lot more men into the show; they could see that he was a big strong lad who got totally swept up by dance, and they realized that loving ballroom dancing didn't make them any less macho.

This year we've extended the series from ten weeks to 12, which means a larger cast, more people to get to know, more training, in fact everything on a grander scale. It's going to be a real test of endurance for the celebrities and professional dancers, and it's even tough for Bruce and me: we really do get involved with the contestants. *Strictly Come Dancing* changes people's lives, it's a very emotional experience, and it's impossible not to get caught up in that emotion. If they're upset, we're upset.

Right now, I'm really looking forward to that moment when the producers unveil the names of the contestants. Bruce and I are like a couple of kids going 'More names! More names!'. You can instantly spot the runners and riders, and you see how people will work together. I can't wait to see who will be doing the dancing this time round – let's hope they know what they're letting themselves in for!

TESS DALY

Series Four

Georgina Bouzova

Exchanging the unflattering uniform of a Casualty *nurse for the glamorous* Strictly Come Dancing *wardrobe is actress, lawyer and kick-boxer Georgina Bouzova.*

Stars of BBC1's medical soaps *Casualty* and *Holby City* haven't done too well on *Strictly Come Dancing*, which says more about their daytime workload than their dancing ability. Will Thorp made it through to the sixth show last year; can Georgina Bouzova, who plays *Casualty*'s Nurse Ellen Zitek, do better? It's not looking good on paper – Bouzova admits that 'I've never learned to dance. I'm a bit self conscious about it, and I always think that everyone else is better than me'.

But she wouldn't be the first absolute beginner to go all the way in the competition, and she certainly makes up for her lack of experience with a steely determination to succeed. 'I'm going to win,' she says. 'There's no point in doing it if you don't want to win. Mind you, it's going to be nerve-wracking. I came to the studio last year when Will [Thorp] was in it, and it looked terrifying. I can't believe that I'm putting myself through it!'.

Bouzova is a quick learner, however, and has a degree in law to prove it. She speaks six languages and lists among her interests kick boxing, yoga, ice skating, roller blading, tennis, tai-chi and horse riding, so she must be fit as well as intelligent. 'I'm throwing myself in at the deep end with the dancing,' she says, 'but that's the best way to learn, and I've got a good teacher. James [Jordan, her partner] says that it's a good way of improving your posture, and I'm also looking forward to being able to get out on the dance floor and impress the boys.'

She's also longing for a chance to look glamorous on screen. 'After two years of playing a nurse, wearing no make-up and scrubs every day, I can't wait to get into some slinky outfits. The costumes are great, the more over-the-top the better. As long as I don't fall over and show my bum, I'll be fine.'

Matt Dawson

*From powerhouse scrum half to elegant ballroom dancer
is one big transformation. Can Matt Dawson make it?*

A familiar face to *A Question of Sport*'s audience – he's a team captain, opposite Ally McCoist – England, Northampton Saints and Wasps rugby star Matt Dawson is stepping well outside his usual sphere for *Strictly Come Dancing*. 'I've never done anything like this,' he says. 'I don't have a burning desire to become a dancer, but the idea of doing something I've never done before in front of a huge live audience is such an adrenalin rush. And it'll give the friends and family something to have a giggle about.'

Dawson retired from rugby in 2006, after a career which earned him 77 England caps and put him in a crucial position for England's victorious performance in the 2003 Rugby World Cup. There's no doubting Dawson's ability as a scrum half – but the rugby pitch is a long way from the ballroom floor. Can Dawson learn grace and accuracy after a career of speed and strength? 'In the last series, Darren Gough came through from just stumbling around on the floor to performing the dances really well, and looking the business, which was just great. I have no idea whether I'm going to be able to do that. At this stage, I've not had a single lesson, so I don't know whether I can pick the steps up or not'

So far, Dawson's dancing has been confined to 'drunken boogies on a Saturday night,' but he hopes to be able to partner his dance-crazy girlfriend from now on. 'I'm not feeling too competitive, but I would like to learn some new skills. As long as I'm not the first out, I'll be happy. Two or three weeks is enough, and anything beyond that is a bonus. I'm looking forward to getting into the costumes; you can't really sign up for *Strictly Come Dancing* and then refuse to wear the sequins and ruffles. When I go down, I want to go down in a blaze of glory!'

Emma Bunton

Emma Bunton really, really wants to learn how to ballroom dance. But will her natural clumsiness and stage fright get the better of her?

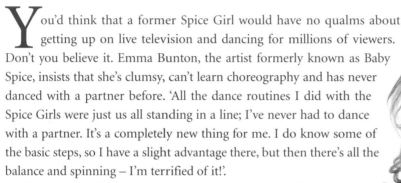

You'd think that a former Spice Girl would have no qualms about getting up on live television and dancing for millions of viewers. Don't you believe it. Emma Bunton, the artist formerly known as Baby Spice, insists that she's clumsy, can't learn choreography and has never danced with a partner before. 'All the dance routines I did with the Spice Girls were just us all standing in a line; I've never had to dance with a partner. It's a completely new thing for me. I do know some of the basic steps, so I have a slight advantage there, but then there's all the balance and spinning – I'm terrified of it!'.

Bunton cheerfully admits to being Clumsy Spice. 'I was always falling over. I fell over in front of thousands of people during the MTV Europe Music Awards one year. I hope I don't do it on *Strictly Come Dancing*, but it's a real possibility. I'm even worried about coming down the stairs. Still, if the worst does happen, I have a plan. I'm just going to blame my partner. I'll say he wasn't holding me up when he should have been.'

Stage fright was a more serious problem in Bunton's Spice Girls career, and she very nearly turned down the *Strictly Come Dancing* job because of her nerves. 'Live performance always affects me very badly, and some people told me that the stress would be too much for me. But I'm not going to let it beat me. I'm determined to go on and do it. It's a very liberating idea: I have no idea of how it's going to go or how long I'll be in the show. There's no fixed schedule. I've just got to get on with it and see how it goes.'

Bunton's been watching *Strictly Come Dancing* since the first series and is a huge fan of Lilia Kopylova. 'I love her. I want to be like her when I dance!' she says. Well, now's her chance: her partner is Lilia's husband, Darren Bennett.

Ray Fearon

Fresh from Kevin Webster's Coronation Street *garage comes Ray Fearon, sometime mechanic, all set to become one of the pin-ups of the new series of* Strictly Come Dancing.

I t's about time *Coronation Street* had some representation in *Strictly Come Dancing*, and the first contender looks as if he might have a good chance at taking the trophy back to Weatherfield. Ray Fearon played heart throb mechanic Nathan Harding from 2005 to 2006; now he's launching his post-soap career by exchanging greasy overalls for skin-tight spandex. 'Nothing can embarrass me when it comes to costumes,' says Feardon, 38. 'There's not much I haven't had to do for my acting. I've worn a thong on stage, I've been sprayed gold, I've had my head shaved, I've grown beards – you name it.'

Fearon's been dancing since his clubbing heyday in the 80s. 'Dancing was such a big part of everyone's social life back then. You went to clubs to dance, and everyone wanted to be the best dancer on the floor. I was never the best, but I certainly wasn't the worst. Since then I've done a bit of training at drama school, and I've had to learn complicated fight choreography for a lot of roles, so I think I'll be able to pick up the steps. It's the same discipline as learning lines, you just have to keep practising till you've got it right.' Fearon also has two distinct physical advantages: he's fit (he's a qualified tennis coach) and flexible, thanks to yoga.

Fearon admits that as soon as he agreed to take part in *Strictly Come Dancing* he started dreading it. 'I'm used to getting on stage and performing in front of people, but that's always in character, never just as Ray. I hope the judges give me constructive criticism. If they tell me what to work on, I'll go away and do it – but if they just tell me I'm rubbish, that won't be enough. I'll want to know why!'.

So what made Fearon take the plunge? 'I wasn't going to do it when they first asked me, but my eight-year-old daughter Rosa May persuaded me. She is a huge fan of the show, and she'd never have forgiven me if I hadn't done it. A few years ago I would never have gone on something like this; I took myself far too seriously. Rosa May has made me lighten up, and I just think about how thrilled she'll be to see me on the show.'

Clare King

Emmerdale's bad girl meets Strictly Come Dancing's *bad boy – will it be murder on the dance floor?*

As Kim Tate, Claire King was the reigning bad girl of *Emmerdale*. Since leaving the show, the actress has starred in prison drama *Bad Girls*, and published an autobiography entitled *Confessions of a Bad Girl*, which shows she takes her hellraising reputation seriously. Therefore King, 42, is delighted to be teamed with Brendan Cole, who's spent three series of *Strictly Come Dancing* carving out his niche as the bad boy of ballroom dancing. 'We can be the bad boy and the bad girl together,' says King. 'It's going to be murder on the dance floor! We have a similar sense of humour, and can take the mickey out of each other, so I think we'll have lots of fun. If he starts shouting, I'll just shout right back.'

Over the course of an acting career that's spanned 20 years, King hasn't had a lot of time for dancing. 'I had the obligatory ballet lessons as a child,' she says, 'and I dance when I'm drunk at parties, but it really isn't my forte. Brendan has really got his work cut out. I wanted to do the show because it's an opportunity to learn a completely new skill. I love the fact that ballroom dancing is such an old-fashioned, polite form of dancing, and it's wonderful that *Strictly Come Dancing* is keeping it alive and reviving it for a new generation.'

Unsurprisingly, King is looking forward to the 'big dramatic numbers' like the Tango. 'I like the dances that you can really get your teeth into. I love drama in performance. Brendan and I are both drama queens,' she says – a statement that Mr Cole might disagree with. 'I love the costumes that go with those numbers. I want them dramatic, over the top, in your face. I really want to go for it. I'll have the wardrobe department slashing them down, slashing them up – anything to distract attention from my dancing! I'm dreading dancing in heels, though. They are going to kill my feet so much.'

Some female contestants have had a rough ride with the judges – but she's not afraid. 'Constructive criticism is water off a duck's back as far as I'm concerned. But if it's below-the-belt bitching, they they'll get it right back in their faces.'

Nicholas Owen

He's more at home reporting from war zones, but the ITV newsman has a secret longing to 'dance down a sweeping staircase with a beautiful girl on my arm'.

Stepping out from behind the newsdesk is ITV anchorman Nicholas Owen who, despite his on-screen gravitas, is actually no stranger to the dance floor. When he's not presenting *News at Ten*, or reporting on wars, royal events or politics, Owen loves nothing better than appearing in pantomimes. 'That usually involves some kind of dance number,' he says, 'but it's always carefully choreographed and then murderously executed. One year I had to do a dance number after a big cake-making scene; the stage was covered in flour and water, and I spent the whole time concentrating on not falling over. It was the worst dance performance I've ever given.'

Now, however, he's ready to take his occasional hoofing to another level. 'Usually I rely on my wife, who's a brilliant dancer; I just follow her lead and hope for the best. But on *Strictly Come Dancing* I'll be getting the best instruction from the best teachers in the world – what more could I hope for? I've always had a dream to learn to tap dance, after watching all those old Fred and Ginger movies, and I'm hoping that this will give me the motivation to do something about that.'

And how does he rate his chances in the competition? 'I have no expectations of hanging on beyond the first show. Just being there for the first one, and than having a jolly good knees-up at the end, is enough for me. I hope people will be kind, but if I'm useless then obviously they'll have to get rid of me. I'm not scared of the judges. You get used to criticism when you're in the public eye. And I've faced Anne Robinson on *The Weakest Link* and escaped in one piece.'

At least Owen, 59, knows that he'll have some dedicated fans in the audience: he has four children and two grandchildren, who will be at home rooting for him.

Louisa Lytton

She's about to leave EastEnders, *where she's played downtrodden Ruby for two years – and Louisa Lytton can't wait to get herself into a more glamorous wardrobe.*

Representing *EastEnders* this year is Louisa Lytton, familiar to Walford-watchers as troubled teen Ruby Allen. She's the youngest of this year's competitors, but she's not going to let that stand in her way. 'Obviously I want to win,' says the plucky 17-year-old. 'I'm quite competitive, and I reckon I'll be okay as long as I keep practising.'

The contrast between the glamour of *Strictly Come Dancing* and life on Albert Square is a big part of the appeal for *EastEnders* stars who sign up to the show. For Lytton, it must come as a great relief, after a couple of years in which Ruby has been involved in disastrous relationships, seen her father sent to prison and struggled to come to terms with her mother and sister being burnt to death. Despite all that, she still managed to be named 'Sexiest Female' at the 2006 Soap Awards. This bodes well for *Strictly Come Dancing.*

'I'm particularly looking forward to getting into the dresses,' she says. 'I just love them – the bright colours, the sparkles, all that. I came to watch the show last year when Patsy Palmer was in it, and the dresses looked so great that I just wanted to get into them right there.'

As a graduate of the Sylvia Young Theatre School, Lytton has some dance training, and is no stranger to the dance floor in her leisure time. 'I love R&B and hip-hop. Anything by Chris Brown will get me up on the dance floor. And I'm always dancing at parties. I think I'm going to enjoy the Latin dances more than the ballroom; they're faster and funker and a bit more me.'

Lytton's only worry at this stage is a slight tendency to clumsiness. 'When I was starting out as an actress, I went on to a film set and walked straight into a camera. I know that there are cameras all over the *Strictly Come Dancing* studio, so I really hope I don't do it again. And I'm worried about how I'll react to the judges: I'm terrified of all of them, and I don't take criticism well. I tend to say what I think, so I'm going to have to learn to keep my big mouth shut.'

Peter Schmeichel

He's a sporting hero to millions. He even has a dog named after him on Coronation Street. *Can hard work and dedicated training turn the huge goalkeeper into a graceful ballroom dancer?*

He's six feet and four inches tall, he's one of the most famous sportsmen ever to work in Britain, but former Manchester United goalkeeper Peter Schmeichel admits that 'I've never danced in my life. Nothing. I was always the one who tried to avoid dancing. I'm a big fellow; I don't feel comfortable on a dance floor.'

So what happened? 'It took a lot of persuasion, and I'm still not sure that I made the right decision. But the first time I thought it might not be such a bad idea was when I took part in a charity football match, and the theme for the wrap party was *Strictly Come Dancing*. In preparation, we all got together and had a lesson for an hour, and I ended up enjoying it so much that I decided to do the show. It made me realise how fit you need to be. I'm always looking for new ways to keep fit, so learning to dance should be quite useful; it will certainly work me hard.'

Schmeichel's sporting career is the stuff of little boys' dreams. As a youngster, he played for a variety of teams at home in Denmark, before being spotted by Alex Ferguson and signed to Manchester United in 1991. It was his contribution to the team that ensured their dominance of the 90s, and the trophies were soon rolling in. When Schmeichel quit in 1999, he went out on a high with Manchester United's legendary treble season. After engagements with Sporting Lisbon, Aston Villa and Manchester City, Schmeichel retired from professional football in 2003.

'I wish I could put my talent for football into this competition,' says Schmeichel, 42. 'If I could do that, I might have a chance of winning. As it is, I'm just going to try and stretch the experience as far as I can, and learn as much as I can. I need a partner who will take no nonsense, who will have a goal and push me towards it. When I train I don't want to mess about, I just want to get on with it.'

Mica Paris

To clubbers and pop fans she's known as a dance diva – but don't be deceived. Mica Paris admits that most of her dancing has been confined to nightclub floors.

As a musician, Mica Paris has the distinct advantage of having a highly developed sense of rhythm – something that not all her fellow competitors are blessed with. She's worked with Prince, Dave Gilmour and a variety of dance and soul producers, and so she's certainly made an awful lot of people get up on the floor – but can she actually do the business herself? 'Despite making a lot of dance records and appearing in West End shows, I've had no dance training at all,' says the 37-year-old singer. 'I love to get up and shake my booty, but that's it. This will be an absolute first for me. And in recent years, I've been so busy that I've not had much chance to dance in clubs; the last time was quite a while ago. Doing *Strictly Come Dancing* will be good for me because it will force me to get up and have a go.'

Mica's big hits, like 'My One Temptation', were in the late 80s and early 90s, but since then she's been far from idle. As well as recording and performing live, she's now an experienced and accomplished broadcaster. She's made a TV series on the history of gospel music, she's presented radio documentaries on Prince and Aretha Franklin, and she regularly hosts her own Radio 2 show *Soul Solutions*, which has a devoted following.

So what would make such a busy career woman want to expose her dance inexperience on live television in front of millions of Saturday-night viewers? 'When I was a child I loved watching *Come Dancing*,' she says. 'People thought I was a freak, and none of my friends watched it, but I loved it. I have no expectations of what the experience is going to be like, but I'm just going to throw myself into it, even if people say I was an idiot to try. It might turn out to be the best thing I've ever done!'

Spoony

No stranger to the dance floor is club DJ Spoony, a man with no fear of sequins and an unlikely passion for golf.

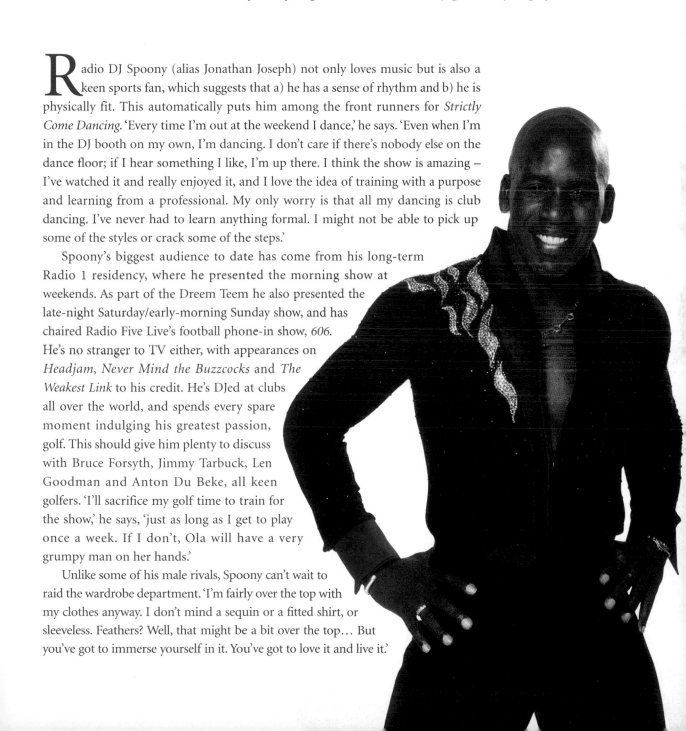

Radio DJ Spoony (alias Jonathan Joseph) not only loves music but is also a keen sports fan, which suggests that a) he has a sense of rhythm and b) he is physically fit. This automatically puts him among the front runners for *Strictly Come Dancing*. 'Every time I'm out at the weekend I dance,' he says. 'Even when I'm in the DJ booth on my own, I'm dancing. I don't care if there's nobody else on the dance floor; if I hear something I like, I'm up there. I think the show is amazing – I've watched it and really enjoyed it, and I love the idea of training with a purpose and learning from a professional. My only worry is that all my dancing is club dancing. I've never had to learn anything formal. I might not be able to pick up some of the styles or crack some of the steps.'

Spoony's biggest audience to date has come from his long-term Radio 1 residency, where he presented the morning show at weekends. As part of the Dreem Teem he also presented the late-night Saturday/early-morning Sunday show, and has chaired Radio Five Live's football phone-in show, *606*. He's no stranger to TV either, with appearances on *Headjam*, *Never Mind the Buzzcocks* and *The Weakest Link* to his credit. He's DJed at clubs all over the world, and spends every spare moment indulging his greatest passion, golf. This should give him plenty to discuss with Bruce Forsyth, Jimmy Tarbuck, Len Goodman and Anton Du Beke, all keen golfers. 'I'll sacrifice my golf time to train for the show,' he says, 'just as long as I get to play once a week. If I don't, Ola will have a very grumpy man on her hands.'

Unlike some of his male rivals, Spoony can't wait to raid the wardrobe department. 'I'm fairly over the top with my clothes anyway. I don't mind a sequin or a fitted shirt, or sleeveless. Feathers? Well, that might be a bit over the top… But you've got to immerse yourself in it. You've got to love it and live it.'

Jan Ravens

She makes a living by impersonating other people – but can Dead Ringers *star Jan Ravens do a convincing portrayal of a ballroom dancer?*

As the star female mimic on BBC2's *Dead Ringers*, Jan Ravens has impersonated Madonna, Beyonce and Gwen Stefani, mean dancers all of them. 'I had to learn a little bit of choreography for all of them,' she says, 'but *Strictly Come Dancing* is completely different. I've got to dance with a partner to fully choreographed routines. Most of my dancing experience has been about getting up on the floor and strutting my funky stuff, which is easy. I'm not self-conscious about it. But I'm really not sure if I'll be able to remember all the steps. My biggest fear is that I'll fall over in the middle of a live routine, or that I'll forget what I'm supposed to be doing. That would be terrible.'

As an experienced actor – as well as *Dead Ringers* she's appeared in dozens of theatre, film and television productions including *Midsomer Murders*, *The Grimleys* and *One Foot in the Grave* – Ravens is looking forward to the dances that involve a bit of characterization. 'I'll feel more at home with the dramatic dances like the Paso Doble, the Tango and the Rumba. I can use my acting skills there, and that will give me a character to hold on to.'

Like many a contestant before her, Ravens approached the costume fittings with a certain amount of trepidation. 'I was very cautious when I went in, asking for subtle colours and conservative cuts. But those costumes are out of this world, and you get carried away. By the end of the fitting I was demanding cerise, amber and lime green dresses, off the shoulder, backless, with as many feathers as possible. My only worry now is the shoes. I'm more of a pit pony than a gazelle, so I will need a bit of a heel.'

Ravens admits that she's usually one of the first to start dancing at a party, and grabs every opportunity to do so. 'The last time I danced was at [*Dead Ringers* co-star] Jon Culshaw's birthday party. I spent the whole night on the dance floor, only to turn around at the end of the evening and see Anton Du Beke standing in the corner. I would never have dared ask him to dance.'

Mark Ramprakash

Fresh from captaining Surrey and notching up a personal best in the process, cricketer Mark Ramprakash is ready for some new challenges. Will he be this season's Darren Gough?

Twelve months ago, you might have said 'A cricketer on *Strictly Come Dancing*? Don't be ridiculous!'. But that was before Darren Gough whirled his way to ballroom glory in the 2005 season and proved that men in white trousers can actually have a sense of rhythm when they step off the pitch.

Mark Ramprakash's life has been entirely dedicated to cricket since the age of 17, when he signed as a professional. Since then he's found fame playing for England, Middlesex, and Surrey, and in 2006 he achieved a career-best score of 301 not out against Northamptonshire. 'I'm 38 this year,' says Ramprakash, 'and I've got to the stage in my life when I want to diversify away from cricket. But when I was initially asked to do the show, I said "no" – it's so far from anything I've ever done before. I like nice normal basic sports like football and golf. But then you look at Darren Gough, and you realize that you might be up to the challenge. Darren made it legit, he made me realize that you could step out of your comfort zone and have fun and see what you could do.'

Like many a male contestant before him, Ramprakash is nervous about the costumes he might be required to wear. 'I'm really not keen on sleeveless shirts,' he says. 'My dress sense is pretty conservative. But the competition will kick in a few weeks down the line, and I suppose if one or two of the outfits are more flamboyant and they want me to wear them, then why not?'

Competition is the key; like all sportsmen, Ramprakash is in it to win it. 'I don't want to be the first out, of course. But this isn't a cricket competition; I'm not going in with the idea that I absolutely have to win, come what may. But I know what it will be like. If I get the through the first few weeks, I'll want to stay in till the end.' Let's hope he does, if only to get back at his eight-year-old daughter. 'She's a big fan of *Strictly Come Dancing*, and when I told her I was going to do the show she couldn't stop laughing. She kept saying "What are you thinking of?"'

Carol Smillie

For Carol Smillie, Changing Rooms *used to be a place where you sawed up MDF and applied emulsion. Now, her changing rooms will be full of false eyelashes and 'bling'.*

As a former recipient of a Rear of the Year Award, Carol Smillie should look pretty good in the *Strictly Come Dancing* wardrobe. 'I'm very excited about the glamour aspect of the show,' she says. 'I love all the false eyelashes, the glitzy costumes. You really can't go into this show with a minimalist attitude. Bling is the name of the game.'

Looking good is only half the battle, however; there's that small detail of actually being able to dance as well. Smillie sums up her dance experience as 'absolutely none whatsoever', although will allow herself to be dragged on to the dance floor at a party, 'usually later in the evening if someone else really insists'. So, while she may have a good rear end in a static position, the big question is: can she shake it?

'I'm worried about the Latin dances, because you really have to strut your stuff, and I'm not at all sure if I have the confidence to do that. I'm quite comfortable about the ballroom dances, because they seem to be much more formulaic. But the Latin numbers are so provocative, which is a worry. I might surprise myself though. I'm going into the competition thinking that I'll get fit and learn something, but you never know what you might discover, do you?'

The former *Changing Rooms* presenter is happy to be in a show that, she says, 'represents what Saturday night TV is really all about. It's good old-fashioned glitz and glamour. My kids will love it, and my dad will love it. I've really enjoyed it myself; I loved watching Colin Jackson in the last series, he was exquisite. Now I've got a chance to be part of it myself.'

Jimmy Tarbuck

He's been entertaining TV audiences for 40 years, but Jimmy Tarbuck is more used to swinging on a golf course than on a dance floor.

Jimmy Tarbuck OBE has been appearing on live television for over 40 years. He's hosted his own shows, he's appeared in front of royalty and he's even followed in Bruce Forsyth's footsteps as the host of *Sunday Night at the London Palladium*. So, in theory, *Strictly Come Dancing* should be like a walk in the park for him. 'I'm looking forward to trying to dance,' he says, 'but that's about as far as it goes. I have absolutely no expectations of winning. I just don't think it's possible.'

Whether that's to do with his age – Tarbuck is 66 – or his lack of dance ability he's not saying, but it certainly can't be for any lack of confidence as an entertainer. He's been performing professionally since the age of 18, worked as a Butlin's Redcoat, and got his own TV series, *It's Tarbuck!*, in 1964, just a year after his first guest appearance on the Palladium show. He's mixed with the good and the great of the show business world, and was honoured in 1994 with an OBE for services to show business and charity. 'So I have no fears,' he says, 'not even of facing the judges. Having met Bruce Forsyth's family on several occasions, nothing scares me.'

Off stage, Tarbuck's great passion is golf: he plays constantly, has written books on the subject, and made TV shows and videos celebrating his favourite sport. He even holds his own tournament, the Jimmy Tarbuck Golf Classic, in either Spain or Portugal every year. He may wish that he'd spent some of that time practising his dancing. 'Most of my dance experience has been social,' he says. 'I've danced in some really memorable places like the *Playboy Club*, *Tramp*, and *Vernon Johnson's Dancing Academy*. Now, the only time I dance is at family weddings. I'm not expecting to reach a high standard. I just want to be part of a piece of great family entertainment.'

James Jordan

He reckons he can take the Strictly Come Dancing *'bad boy' crown away from Brendan Cole – but his wife will be watching from the wings.*

Latin American champions James and Aleksandra 'Ola' Jordan have been dancing together for six years – and they're partners off the dance floor too. 'I won't change my attitude towards her just because we're on television competing against each other,' he says. 'In some ways, I'd prefer her to do better than me; she's my baby and I love her, so I want her to do really well.'

Jordan (28) grew up in Kent and has been dancing since he was 13, when his sister Kelly dragged him along to classes. By 14 he was entering competitions, and by 18 he was winning them. After a successful career as an under-21, he 'retired' for a while, split with his partner and contemplated his future. 'I was fed up with dancing, and needed a break. Then I went to Poland for a try-out with Ola, and she was

perfect for me.' The couple danced together professionally for two years before marrying in 2003, then moved to Hong Kong where Jordan embarked on a lucrative teaching career. 'In Hong Kong, I can teach very few students and get paid an awful lot of money for it. My main student is a 62-year-old lady who looks and dances like a 40-year-old. She was happy to let me go for three months to live my dream!'

Jordan describes himself as 'honest and straightforward' and says he won't tolerate any laziness from his celebrity student. He's also determined to win. 'I'm not a nice boy, and I think sometimes bad boys do well with the public. If anyone says they aren't in it to win it, they're lying.' So watch out, Georgina Bourzova – you may be in for a bumpy ride!

Aleksandra 'Ola' Jordan

Mrs Jordan says she's 'terrified' of the Strictly Come Dancing *experience – but once she gets on the dance floor she's counting on her Latin passion to see her through.*

Aleksandra Jordan, known as Ola, won the Open Championships at home in Poland at the age of 17, and went on to be placed in the world top 12 in 1999. She was at the top of her game – but then she split from her partner and started looking around for fresh fields to conquer. Enter James Jordan, also footloose and fancy-free – they clicked immediately. Ola (now 24) moved to England in 2000, married Jordan and followed him to Hong Kong. 'Now I'm looking forward to appearing on TV with my husband,' she says, 'as long as he's not paired with a beautiful model! I don't think we'll fight about who is better, but that doesn't mean that I don't want to beat him. He might do better than me because of his very strong personality – I'm much more quiet and shy off the dancefloor, and much less competitive than he is. But I'm going to try very hard.' After moving to Hong Kong,

the Jordans took a break from competitive dancing, and re-entered the fray in 2005. The *Strictly Come Dancing* gig has reawakened her sporting spirit. 'I'm very excited about what lies ahead, but also terrified because I just don't know what to expect. Whether I'm successful or not lies hugely with the celebrity I get – they will either make life very easy or very difficult for me. I'd like to get a singer – they have musicality, and it would be easy to teach them the rhythmical elements of a dance. Ideally I'd like Robbie Williams. He's got it all – youth, talent, rhythm, and he's very famous, which helps!'. Instead, she's got Spoony, who may not be quite as famous as Robbie, but scores high in all the other categories.

Vincent Simone

Bringing an authentic Latin flavour to the 2006 competition is Italian heart throb Vincent Simone. But will he know who any of the British celebrities are?

Vincent Simone started dancing at the age of five. 'I would dance at any party we went to,' he says. 'Dancing is such a massive part of Italian life, so it was bound to happen. I would dance at any party; my mother said I was born to perform.' By the age of seven, Simone was taking dance lessons near the family home on the south coast of Italy, and took part in his first competition aged nine. He won, and the following year became the Juvenile Italian Champion. Astonishingly, he was teaching professionally at the age of 12. 'My parents opened a dance school, and I just loved teaching. By the age of 14, I had couples in the Italian and regional championships.' There was only so far Simone could go in Italy, though, and soon he was looking for a bigger stage. 'I realized that if I wanted to make it professionally, I needed to move. So at 17 I came to Surrey and found Flavia.' Flavia Cacace became his partner both on and off the dance floor, and they've been together for ten years. Simone's favourite dances are the Rumba and the Argentine Tango, which he loves because they are 'passionate and seductive'. Sounds promising… 'I love passion. I don't want to hear any moaning from my partner about what they can and can't do – I just want passion for the dance. I'm an outrageous flirt too, so she'd better watch out! And of course, being a typical Italian man I love fast, flash cars. My dream is to own a Ferrari, so who knows – if I'm partnered with a very rich celebrity, maybe she'll buy me one!'. Louisa Lytton is only 17, however, so Simone may have to wait a little longer for the Ferrari.

Flavia Cacace

From Naples, by way of Guildford, Flavia Cacace is an expert in the Argentine Tango and is looking for a partner who can match her passion for dance.

Like her partner Vincent Simone, Flavia Cacace was born in southern Italy, but moved with her family to the UK when she was four years old when her father joined a family business in Surrey. The youngest of six children, she started dancing at the age of six at a Saturday morning class in Guildford, and began a rapid rise through the competitive ranks. 'Mum and Dad spent so long taxiing me around to rehearse,' she says. 'They were so supportive. I couldn't have done it without their support.' Just after taking her GCSEs, Cacace met another young Italian who, like her, was looking for a new partner. 'Vincent and I were both taking lessons from the same teacher, and it was suggested we should have a try-out together. It worked perfectly. It's a complete

coincidence that we are both from Italy; we met in Guildford!' Cacace stayed on at college to do her A levels, and financed her dancing through part-time jobs; in 2001 she and Simone turned professional. They've been teaching and performing ever since. 'I'm not too bothered who I teach as long as they are enthusiastic,' she says. 'I would love someone who is lively and enjoys life – the more fun we can have the better. The ideal celebrity for me would be a comedian, someone light-hearted who can make me laugh, like Jonathan Ross or Joe Pasquale. As long as they haven't got two left feet, we'll be able to do anything!' She's in luck: Jimmy Tarbuck's been making the world laugh for several decades, and is no stranger to the old soft-shoe shuffle. Cacace's only real worry is getting used to working without Vincent. 'We've always danced together and it will take a bit of getting used to. I don't think we'll be competitive with each other, but once I'm up there I'm fighting for myself and my partner.'

Series Four
The Couples

The Presenters

'Our job is to bring the party into everyone's living room on a Saturday night,' says Tess Daly, co-presenter of *Strictly Come Dancing*. 'I see every aspect of the show: I'm out front with Bruce; I'm with the celebrities and the dancers, seeing their backstage jitters; I see the hair and make-up and wardrobe, and the most gratifying thing is seeing it all come together live, although I've probably seen more panic attacks than anyone else involved in the programme.'

For Daly and Bruce Forsyth, taking on the job of presenting *Strictly Come Dancing* was as much a leap of faith as for any of the contestants. They were going to be carrying an untried format; if it fell flat, they would be left with egg on their faces. 'Of course, we had no idea that the show would take off in the way it did,' says Forsyth, 'but we had faith. I wouldn't have done it otherwise. There's always an element of anxiety about a new format, but you have to go out there and sell it, get it across to the audience. From my point of view, it was good from the start, because there's plenty of opportunity for banter with the audience, with the dancers and with the judges. But it wasn't until the third or fourth week of the first series that the competitive side really got going, and then I knew we had a winner on our hands.'

Nobody saw the competition at such close quarters as Tess Daly. Interviewing the contestants backstage before they went on, or after they had performed, she witnessed the highs and lows of what quickly became a very intense experience for all concerned. 'Just before they go on to dance, we play the video of their week's training – and it's the first time they've seen it. Everyone crowds around backstage to see what the others have been up to, and that's when the competition really hots up. I've heard a lot of backbiting comments, nothing terribly bitchy, but you quickly realize that these people are serious about winning. Then, when they have to go on, the tension is incredible. I've never seen such fear. The celebrities are having to do something that doesn't come naturally to them, they've got to do it live in front of millions of people, and everything rests on that 90-second performance. That's their one chance. I really feel for them.'

'The element of competition is vital,' says Forsyth. 'You've got a group of people who may never have danced a step in their lives – they might muck around in a disco from time to time but that's about it – and they don't want to go out there looking like a fool. They want to win. They start watching each other's performances, seeing who's got the edge in the Quickstep or the Tango. The athletes in particular are very competitive; that's the way they work. Denise Lewis had no dance background at all, but she was a very fit, conditioned woman who was determined to work on her technique until she felt she could win.'

Both Forsyth and Daly have their favourite moments from the competition: Christopher Parker running around with Hanna Karttunen on his back in the Paso Doble, Julian Clary shaking his maracas in Blackpool, but the story that most stands out for both of them is the transformation of Natasha Kaplinsky. 'That was the most outstanding thing about the first series,' says Daly, 'watching Natasha turn from this terrified woman who was literally shaking with fear backstage into an elegant, confident dancer who could win the competition.'

'Natasha was petrified at first,' says Forsyth. 'She actually said to me backstage, "Bruce, please can you make sure that I get knocked out in the first week?" But then she started to enjoy herself, she realized that she could dance and she just romped away. That gave out such a positive message to people, showing that you can overcome your fears or your lack of experience and turn them into a real achievement – and that's exactly what *Strictly Come Dancing* is all about.'

And of course Kaplinsky enjoyed *Strictly Come Dancing* so much that, when Tess Daly was obliged to take time off to have a baby, she came in to present much of the second series. 'That was the best part of the whole experience for me,' she says, 'because I was back in my comfort zone! To be honest, I really enjoyed seeing other people go through the terror that I'd experienced. You could see them going on the same journey, all the fear about performing, all the physical discomfort, the anxiety at the time of voting, which is absolutely hideous, and you could think, "My God, I did all that!" Looking back on it, I found it hard to believe that I'd really put myself through it.'

But it was Kaplinsky's initial fear that endeared her to audiences and did as much to win her the first series as her evident dancing ability. 'The judges give their scores on technique, but the audience is responding to personality as well,' says Forsyth. 'I realized that during the first series, when somehow Christopher Parker was coming back week after week because all the mums and young girls were voting for him. They could see how hard he was trying, and how upset he was when the judges were mean to him, and they wanted to give the poor lad another

chance. Our job as presenters is to mediate between the expert opinions of the judges and the sympathies of the audience. That part of the show when the contestants come up and face the judges has become the moment when it all crystallises. The dancers have a chance to answer back, and emotions run high. The judges aren't afraid of being controversial or upsetting the dancers; they have to maintain their standards. I have to remind the audience of that sometimes, when they start booing: the judges are judging the dance, not the person. They're professionals. The public always has the chance to have their say, and that tension between the two voting systems is what's made *Strictly Come Dancing* such a success.'

The presenters' job doesn't just begin and end with the Saturday night show; *Strictly Come Dancing* makes almost as many demands on their time as it does on the dancers'. 'We spend three days in the week preparing, watching the films of rehearsals as much as possible, meeting with the producer, discussing the scripts, meeting with the band and practising our little dance routine that we do at the bottom of the steps. That has to be right, or we're going to look very bad! Anton [du Beke] has given me a couple of lessons; I want to look the part.'

'Saturday is a very long day,' says Forsyth, 'what with the results show later in the evening as well. By the time I get home I'm exhausted. Sundays are a

bit of a write-off. I get up in time for Sunday lunch, then I spend the afternoon reading the papers and sleeping. I've always appreciated lazy Sundays at home, ever since doing *Sunday Night at the London Palladium* for all those years in the 50s and 60s.'

For Forsyth and Daly, the experience of presenting *Strictly Come Dancing* has been entirely positive. 'All I ever get is positive remarks,' says Forsyth. 'I was doing a phone-in show on Radio 5 Live last year, and a woman called in to say how much her children loved it. They were three and four years old, and she said that from the moment they got up in the morning till they went to bed at night, they were fighting – apart from when *Strictly Come Dancing* came on, and then they were dancing together. That says it all for me.'

For Daly, the *Strictly Come Dancing*-effect has gone even further. 'I was three months' pregnant when the first series started, then I gave birth to my daughter, Phoebe, towards the end of 2004. I went back to present some of the second series when she was six weeks old, and she celebrates her first birthday at the start of the third series. She really is a *Strictly Come Dancing* baby, and everyone involved in the show has become like family to us. When I took her in to meet everyone, the wardrobe department gave her a little Paso Doble cape with her initial 'P' on the back. That's how much the show means to us all.'

It Takes Two
Claudia Winkleman

It Takes Two, the week-day evening show that follows the contestants and judges through the course of the series, has become an integral part of the *Strictly Come Dancing* experience. 'It's got a following in its own right,' says presenter Claudia Winkleman. 'We manage to get closer to the people than you can manage in the Saturday night show. There's more time for the judges to explain why they gave a certain score, or for the celebrities and the professionals to talk about a certain step, or the problems they're having. I just hang around them the whole time, soaking it all up.' Winkleman was recruited to take over *It Takes Two* in the second series, and admits it was her dream job. 'They called me up and said "celebrities, dancing, sequins, daily show," and I did a one-woman Mexican wave. I loved the first series, and now I'm totally obsessed by the whole process. I don't leave those people alone from the minute they arrive at the studio. I follow them into make-up. I can't get enough of it.'

Like everyone involved in the *Strictly Come Dancing* phenomenon, Winkleman's been swept up in the dedication that everyone brings to the contest. 'My only worry when I started the job was that the celebrities wouldn't take it very seriously, and that we wouldn't have much to talk about. But in fact, they nearly all start to love dancing. Obviously the professionals are 100 per cent dedicated, but by the time you're a few weeks into the series, so are the

celebrities. It's not just the feathers and sequins, it's the discipline of the training as well. I just have to swan in and put on the eyelashes and start filming; for the contestants, it absorbs their whole lives. Even the ones that don't have natural dance ability, like Fiona Phillips and Diarmuid Gavin, have to summon up incredible courage to put themselves on the line in that way.'

It Takes Two is filmed at a studio in Covent Garden, and the contestants will often book a rehearsal space nearby in order to facilitate popping in. 'They tell me everything,' says Winkleman, 'from "I've lost two stone" to "I can't master the Tango". There's so much to talk about, we find it hard to stop. I got so carried away with Bill Turnbull discussing his Viennese Waltz, the cleaners actually had to ask us to leave the studio. The professionals and the judges are great, and they have really deepened the way people understand the dances.'

And isn't Winkleman itching to get out on the dance floor herself? 'I've got my hands full with the daily show, and with two small children at home,' she says. 'And one thing I've realized is just how exhausting the dancing can be. I used to think it was just something you did at a club – a couple of vodka tonics and a spot of robotics round your handbag. But these people are athletes; it's a very serious commitment, and any celebrity that comes into the show thinking it's going to be a breeze is in for a rude awakening.'

'There's more time for the judges to explain why they gave a certain score, or for the celebrities and the professionals to talk about a certain step, or the problems they're having'

Here Comes

Meet the people in power: the experts who can make all the training worthwhile, or can send the defeated contestants back to the dressing room...

Craig Revel Horwood

BACKGROUND Craig started as a dancer at home in Australia before moving to London and choreographing extensively for the West End stage. His many credits include the Olivier-nominated *Spend Spend Spend*. He also runs a furniture shop.

HIGHEST SCORE 10 to Jill in the series-two final, and Darren in the series-three final

LOWEST SCORE 1 to Quentin in series two and to Fiona in series three

WATCHES OUT FOR Personality (or lack of it)

MOST LIKELY TO SAY 'It's meant to be the dance of love, but it seemed as though it was the dance of desperation.'

Arlene Phillips

BACKGROUND One of Britain's best-known choreographers, Arlene made her name as the creator of 70s dance troupe Hot Gossip. She went on to choreograph *Saturday Night Fever* for the West End and Broadway, plus countless feature films and music videos for Queen, Elton John, Robbie Williams and many others.

HIGHEST SCORE Gave the show's first ever 10 to Natasha in series one, also to Jill and Denise in series two and Zoe, Colin, James and Darren in series three

LOWEST SCORE 1 to Quentin in series two

WATCHES OUT FOR Professional attitude, expressiveness in performance

MOST LIKELY TO SAY 'Where was the sex?'

the Judge

Len Goodman

BACKGROUND Len has been dancing all his adult life, and he now lectures and judges all over the world as well as running a dance school in Kent. But it nearly didn't happen: he started out determined to be a professional footballer.

HIGHEST SCORE 10 to Jill in the series-two final, and to Colin, Darren, James and Zoe in series three

LOWEST SCORE 3 to Quentin in the first show of series two

WATCHES OUT FOR Technique, good basic choreography and sticks to the rules

MOST LIKELY TO SAY 'You don't have to break the rules. I'm going to have to drop a point.'

Bruno Tonioli

BACKGROUND Long ago, Bruno was one of Bruce Forsyth's dancers and competed in *A Song for Europe* before starring in Elton John's 'I'm Still Standing' video and establishing himself as a choreographer. He's worked with Michael Jackson, Paul McCartney and French and Saunders.

HIGHEST SCORE 10 to Jill and Denise in the series-two final, and to Zoe, Colin and Darren in series three

LOWEST SCORE 3 to Quentin in series two and Fiona in series three

WATCHES OUT FOR A strong, storytelling relationship between the dancers

MOST LIKELY TO SAY 'It was like watching a Robin Reliant competing with a Ferrari.'

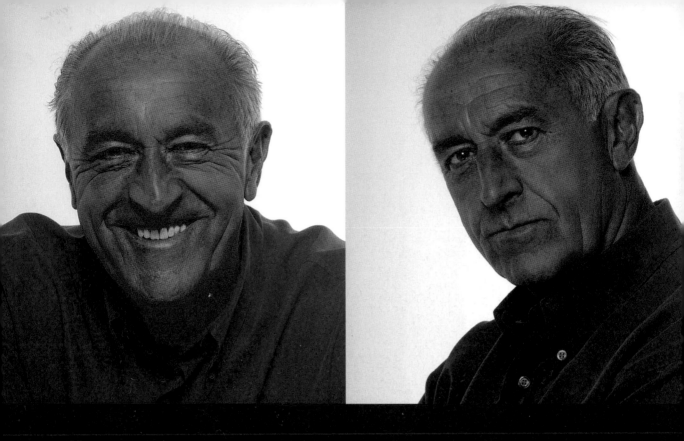

L en Goodman is the linchpin of *Strictly Come Dancing* – the man with the most experience of the ballroom and Latin-American worlds, a dancer, teacher and judge who brings technical and professional credibility to the show. 'When we were first talking about the format,' he says, 'there were a lot of people in the ballroom world who were miffed because there weren't going to be four professional ballroom judges on the panel. I had misgivings myself, I confess. But as the show got going, I realized that it worked. If there were four people like me, you'd get four identical scores, all based on technique. But with Arlene, Craig and Bruno you're getting a score based on a different approach. I'm looking at steps and holds – but Bruno is looking at the quality of the performance, Craig's looking for interaction and line, and Arlene is looking at the choreographic elements. There's no point in judging non-dancers purely on technique, it wouldn't be fair. We have to look at all the qualities that they bring to a performance.'

The tension between the stern verdict of the judges and the response of the voting audience is what makes *Strictly Come Dancing* tick – and that's something the judges are well aware of. 'We get a lot of flak from audiences who think we're being mean to their favourite celebrity, but I have to keep stressing that we're voting with our heads. It's up to the audience to vote with their hearts. We can only judge the dancing as it's done on the night – we're not looking at rehearsals or training or backstage footage. I've got a responsibility to the dance world to make sure that the best technique gets the best mark. It's not always easy, because obviously we're not seeing them all dancing together at the same time, so we can't rank them against each other. You have to start off giving average marks – sixes and sevens – until you get an idea of the overall standard, then you can start giving higher or lower marks as they're deserved.

'First of all, I'd be looking for decent posture, because if you've got that, you're halfway to being able to dance. Some people just don't have it, and you

know that they'll never be able to do more than just flap around on the floor. Then I look at the footwork, which is the basis of the dance. If the footwork's good, you can build up the choreography, but if it's not there, then it's like building a house without strong foundations – the walls are going to fall down. Finally, I look at the choreography, which should turn it all into a performance. A dance is like a garden: you've got to have the basic things, such as the grass and the trees – that's the posture and the footwork – but you also need the flowers, and that's the choreography. I know I come out with a lot of funny comments and analogies sometimes, about sausages and sizzle and all that, but all I'm trying to say is that you have to mix basic steps with good performance.'

Goodman has been such a success on *Strictly Come Dancing* that he was invited to judge the American version of the show, *Dancing with the Stars*. 'They called me up on the Friday, and said, "Would you be prepared to fly out to Los Angeles on Monday for a show that starts on Tuesday?" I nearly didn't go,

but I'm glad I did, because *Dancing with the Stars* turned out to be the biggest entertainment show on American television in years. The attention it got was incredible: there were six or seven network-news teams hanging around at the end of every broadcast, wanting to interview us. But I was stuck out there for seven weeks, getting homesick, so I was pleased when it was all over.'

Now Goodman and the rest of the panel are poised to deliver their verdict on another crop of celebrities – and he's coming to terms with a certain amount of fame himself. 'It's nice to be recognized, and people are never nasty to me because they think I'm a kind judge. Craig's the one who gets it in the neck – he's been accosted on trains and given a very hard time by people who think he's Mr Mean. It's nice for me to have a bit of fame, and it's done wonders for the dance business as a whole – but it's not going to turn my head. I was 60 when I got this job, and I'd been round the block a few times, so this is just the icing on the cake.'

The Dancers

The professional dancers have the hardest job on Strictly Come Dancing. *They're not just responsible for getting onto the studio floor week in, week out, performing effortlessly elegant, exciting dances and putting up with the sometimes unkind remarks of the judges, but they also have to train celebrities who, let's face it, may not have a natural aptitude for dancing.*

They also have to choose music for each dance, create choreography to make the most of their partner's ability, and co-ordinate costume and make-up into a single entity that will, hopefully, get them through to the following week's show.

'We're pretty competitive,' says Anton du Beke, now dancing into a fourth series of the show. 'We have to be, because in the professional dance world you won't get anywhere without a competitive streak. So we're very committed to practising, just like any athlete, and we have to be on top of every aspect of the performance. When we signed up to do the first series, we were only contracted to rehearse for six hours a week. It ended up being six hours a day, or more. We had to fit around the celebrities' lives; in my case that meant following Lesley Garrett on her tour all over the country, fitting in rehearsals when we could. We all realized that we had to put the hours in, otherwise we'd have nothing to make a show out of come Saturday.'

The dancers are dedicated – but what about the celebrities? 'You can tell straight away if you've got something decent to work with,' says Darren Bennett, who partnered Jill Halfpenny to victory in the second series. 'Jill and I first met in a photographic studio, and as she took my hand I could feel her body weight – which means that she's conscious of where her body is in space. I asked her to extend a foot, and she did it instantly. I knew then that we had the potential to go all the way in the show, because she had innate ability. If someone can feel rhythm, count beats, and knows where their limbs are in relation to each other, you can teach them to dance. If they can't do those things, there's not a lot you can do.

You can coach them to repeat sequences of steps, but they'll never dance. We see that all the time as teachers, and I think the viewers can see it on screen. Some of the celebrities literally could not hear rhythm. And we can't teach that. You've either got it or you haven't.' Rehearsing

became the most intense part of the *Strictly Come Dancing* experience for many of the professionals. 'We start five weeks before the first show,' says du Beke, 'and we develop a close relationship very quickly. You have to. Dance is very physical, and these people are learning from scratch, so they have to be able to take criticism. My job as a teacher is to give criticism without destroying the ego, and to send them out there feeling like a million dollars. That wasn't difficult with Lesley because she loved to dance and had natural ability. It was harder with Esther [Rantzen, in series two] because she had so much to learn. Esther is a woman and a half, but steps sort of elude her. I realized that she was going to be stepping out onto the studio floor, dressed in a revealing frock, dancing a Samba and being judged against someone like Sarah Manners, who looks like a supermodel. I had to give her the confidence to go out there feeling equal, with her own sexuality, her own charisma, that people would respond to. She underwent a metamorphosis that was extraordinary for a 64-year-old woman.'

'As dancers, we were all committed to making the show look as good as possible,' says Darren Bennett. 'I was staying up all night to get the choreography finished in time. Arlene Phillips once complimented me on a piece of choreography; little did she know that I'd sketched it out in my front room the night before, dancing round the furniture. The

deadlines can get very hairy, and that's when your relationship with your celebrity really matters. If they can't take criticism, you're sunk. Luckily for me, Jill and I spoke our minds and swore at each other, and we didn't care. Because she's an actor, she understands that you have to get it right. None of us wanted to be involved in anything that would make ballroom look kitsch or silly. We get enough of that prejudice, and this was a chance to set the record straight.'

While everyone realized that *Strictly Come Dancing* could do just that, there was uncertainty right until the show was on air. 'It was a leap of faith,' says Anton du Beke, 'Live, ballroom dancing is wonderful and exciting – you've got gorgeous men and women, great dresses and incredible athleticism – but it can look cheesy on television, as we know from *Come Dancing*. It was important that people understood just how hard it is, like any sport. There was a moment in the first series when we all started taking it very seriously – it was, I think, the defining moment for the show. It was the first time anyone had been knocked out. We'd all been working so hard to get it on, we didn't think about results, and then we lost Jason [Wood] and Kylie [Jones]. There were a lot of tears – partly of relief, but also of sadness, because we realized that we might be next. That's when everyone dug in, and the show really took flight.'

History of the Show

Everyone remembers the television series Come Dancing – *those stiff, smiling mannequins gliding round the ballroom floor in yards of tuile and black penguin suits, the Rumbas, the Cha Cha Chas, the wonderful provincial Britishness of it all. But when the axe finally fell on* Come Dancing *in 1995 after years of dwindling audiences, it would have been a brave soul indeed who could have predicted that, less than a decade later, the format would have been made over into the biggest entertainment hit on British television in years.*

'It was one of those ideas that came about quite unexpectedly,' says Karen Smith, Creative Head of Format Entertainment. 'They were all sitting round in a commissioning meeting at BBC1, talking about celebrity programmes and new formats, and the entertainment commissioning executive said, "Why don't we bring back *Come Dancing* – but with celebs?" Everyone laughed at first, but the more they thought about it the more they liked it – and that's when I was brought in.'

Smith came from a solid background in light-entertainment events – she'd produced *Comic Relief Does Fame Academy* for the BBC and *The Games*, a celebrity-athletics contest, for Channel 4. 'I knew absolutely nothing about the dance world,' she says, 'but that didn't seem to matter. What I did know about was doing big, live-TV events with a competition element. The rest I could learn.'

That was in autumn 2003 – which gave Smith and her team only 24 weeks in which to put the show together from scratch. There was no format and no team – just a conviction that the combination of old-fashioned dancing and new-style celebrity competition would work. 'I had faith in the idea from the beginning,' says Smith, 'because it seemed to appeal to such a wide range of people. We knew we were aiming for the Saturday-evening slot, the Holy Grail of scheduling, and the potential audience is enormous. Everyone from eight to 80 is available in theory, so if a show's going to work in that slot it has to appeal right across the board. I knew that the celebrity aspect would get the 20- and 30-something audience hooked. The music and dancing would appeal to the older audiences. And then there were the spangly frocks, the Barbie-Doll quality that would bring in the little girls.'

Confident that *Pro-Celebrity Come Dancing*, as it was then called, worked in theory, Smith set about devising a format that would combine the competitive edge of *Pop Idol* and the breathtaking skill of the professional dance world. She contacted dancers and judges, she went to competitions around

> *'Why don't we bring back* Come Dancing *– but with celebs?'*

the country and immersed herself in the strange new world of ballroom and Latin. She watched tapes of the old *Come Dancing* series to see what, if anything, could be salvaged from a seemingly outdated formula. And, crucially, she worked out a voting system that would give equal weight to professional judges and viewing public. 'That's a difficult balancing act. If you give all the power to the viewers, like in *Pop Idol*, then there's going to be a landslide win for someone regardless of their dancing skills; they'll get votes because they're popular. If the pro judges have all the power, then the viewers have no input. That was the problem with *Come Dancing*; you just saw these one-dimensional figures, you knew nothing about them, there was no

Over the 50s and 60s, Come Dancing *was the darling of British light entertainment and drew in huge audiences on a regular basis. Eventually, though, the times caught up with it and the dated-looking programme was axed in 1995.*

reason to feel involved. The dancers just seemed like bizarre comedy people; you didn't see behind the façade. By working out a voting system that gives equal weight to the judges and the viewers, we ensure that the contestants are marked for their dancing ability and for their personality. That's the key to the show's success. It doesn't alienate the serious dance fans, and it draws in that big Saturday-night audience.'

'We knew it was a winner, but we knew it was going to be a hard sell, so we made a point of turning up at all the pitching meetings with a couple of dancers in tow'

Stepping out: Tess Daly and Bruce Forsyth head up the dancers and celebrities involved in the first series.

The next step was casting the professional dancers. There were eight in the first series, four men and four women – and they had to be the best in the business in order to give *Strictly Come Dancing* the credibility it would need to attract celebrity contestants. 'I had no idea at first just how famous these people were,' says Smith. 'They could be the world champion, but they could walk down the street in Britain and no one would know them. They're incredibly famous in Japan and America, where ballroom dancing is taken very seriously – but here they're only known by the real hardcore. Most of them live in flats and semis in south-east London, because that's where the best teachers are – but in

Japan they're mobbed by huge screaming crowds. When Donnie Burns, the 14-times world Latin champion, visited Japan recently, he outsold Prince at the Tokyo Dome!'

With her format and her dancers in place, Smith, the Head of Format Entertainment and the Format Entertainment Development team set about selling the project to BBC1, BBC3 and BBC Worldwide, who would be screening or selling the show all over the world. 'We knew it was a winner, but we knew it was going to be a hard sell, so we

'I knew we had to have someone for everyone. I really wanted Christopher Parker, because he was in a famous soap, the young girls love him'

made a point of turning up at all the pitching meetings with a couple of dancers in tow. We'd outline the format, so they could see it was rock-solid, then we'd unleash the dancers. As soon as you see them in action, it's breathtaking. It clinched it every time.'

And then came the really hard part: casting the celebrities. They had to be famous; there's no point in putting on a Saturday-night celebrity show with a bunch of people nobody's heard of. They had to commit themselves to 13 weeks of hard physical work for an untried format that looked, on paper, like a bizarre collision of the kitsch and the passé. Smith drew up a shortlist and set about wooing them.

Putting on the Ritz: a newly suave Christopher Parker prepares to brush the dust of Walford from his shoes.

'I knew we had to have someone for everyone. I really wanted Christopher Parker, because he was in a famous soap, the young girls love him and so do the mums and grandmas. Martin Offiah is a big, tough rugby player, and he made it OK for men to watch. Claire Sweeney has that girl-next-door thing. Lesley Garrett brought in an older, more highbrow audience. And David Dickinson ticks every single box; he even gets the student. It sounds quite calculated, but you have to be.'

'It's become exactly what a Saturday-night show should be – it's a safe place where nothing bad will happen, a little piece of magic'

The mix of personalities has become the key to the show – and half the fun in *Strictly Come Dancing* lies in looking at the list of contestants for each new series and wondering who'll surprise the audience. In the second series, Julian Clary broke away from the pack to become the unexpected favourite, transcending all the rules on sheer force of personality alone. But it was series three that, perhaps, contained the biggest surprise of all, as the male celebrities pulled ahead of the women not just with the viewers, but with the judges as well. Everyone suspected that Colin Jackson would be able to dance – but Darren Gough? 'He turned out to be one of the most memorable *Strictly Come Dancing* stories of all,' says series producer Sam Donnelly. 'He started off thinking "this will be a bit of fun", but then he got bitten by the dancing bug. After three or four shows, it became apparent that he was taking it very seriously, that he'd been looking at Len's dance tips on the Internet and was getting quite competitive. In the first two series, a couple of favourites emerged early on and they were either brilliant dancers or great personalities that the public loved. But in series three, the quality of the dancing was generally much higher, and that was what the final was all about. Nobody could guess who would win in the final; Darren, Zoe and Colin had all gone on such amazing journeys and discovered real talent within themselves.'

As *Strictly Come Dancing* progresses, the expectations placed upon it become higher. After the first series, Karen Smith and her team were given just 16 weeks to put the second series together. There were more dancers, more episodes, more of everything.

The third series was bigger still, and the fourth series will have 14 couples coming down the staircase in the first episode. Spin-offs, like Claudia Winkleman's *It Takes Two* show, have become huge ratings-winners in their own right. The brand shows no sign of slowing down, and now *Strictly Come Dancing* is essential to BBC1's Saturday-night line-up.

If channel bosses were surprised, the creators certainly weren't. '*Strictly Come Dancing* has become exactly what a Saturday-night show should be,' says Karen Smith. 'It's a safe place where nothing bad will happen, a little piece of magic. You can sit down with your children or your grandmother, and you know it's going to be glamorous, glitzy, funny, dramatic, tense and thoroughly entertaining. The competition element means it never gets dull, the music and dancing and design make it gorgeous to look at, and the personalities draw you in. And it has to work on a more sophisticated level too; there has to be just the right element of tongue-in-cheek humour about it to put it across in the 21st century. I never wanted it to be camp or parodic, but there has to be a bit of good-natured irony. You can have a laugh about it, but you can enjoy it for what it is at the same time.'

History of Come Dancing

BBC Television had only just been back in business after the War when it launched *Come Dancing* in October 1949. It was the brainchild of Eric Morley, a young, freshly demobbed impresario who had just got a job with dance promoters Mecca – and who, thanks to *Come Dancing* and *Miss World*, would become one of the most powerful men in British variety in the 60s and 70s. *Come Dancing* started off as a live broadcast from regional ballrooms around the country, where couples would compete while professional dancers Syd Perkins and Edna Duffield gave tips and teaching advice. The first show was from the Manchester Ritz Ballroom; within a year, it was an established hit, and soon dropped the educational slant to become a straightforward competition. In 1953, the long-lasting format of regional heats and a national final was introduced.

Morley was the show's original master of ceremonies, but he was eventually supplanted by a string of celebrity presenters – and over the years they included Terry Wogan, Angela Rippon, Judith Chalmers, Keith Fordyce, Rosemarie Ford, Brian Johnston, Michael Aspel, David Jacobs and even Noel Edmonds.

Over the years, *Come Dancing* tried to keep up with the times, introducing rock 'n' roll dancing in the 50s, even disco in the 70s – but in the end it seemed terminally old-fashioned. It was moved to later and later slots, audiences declined, and it was finally axed in 1995.

International Versions

The success of *Strictly Come Dancing* sparked an extraordinary scramble for foreign rights to the show, and now audiences around the world have become immersed in the finer points of ballroom dancing. 'It's taken me completely by surprise,' says Creative Head of Format Entertainment Karen Smith. 'The format has sold all over Europe, in America and Australia, and Japan'.

The American version, *Dancing with the Stars*, played to enormous audiences on ABC, and was their biggest entertainment show for years. The first series was won by *General Hospital* star Kelly Monaco, and the second series, in 2006, by former boyband member and Broadway actor Drew Lachey. In Australia, the show was such a success that Channel Seven ran two series back to back.

Production and Location

The gorgeous dance hall that we see every week on Strictly Come Dancing *looks like everyone's fantasy of the perfect nightclub: a huge floor accessed by a sweeping staircase, a glamorous bandstand, lights, curtains, arches and an audience seated at tables and chairs. But it's all an illusion; it's actually a set that comes to pieces after every show and is stashed away in a corner of BBC Television Centre in West London.*

The lights return to the warehouse, the curtains are folded, the chairs stacked. Even the dance floor breaks up into dozens of pieces, waiting for the following week when the whole thing is slowly, laboriously and painstakingly reassembled, and the illusion begins all over again.

The first question that everyone asks is, 'Why?' Wouldn't it just be easier to build a semi-permanent set that lasts for the duration of the series, thus avoiding the time, labour and expense of striking, storing and rebuilding it after every show? The answer, incredibly, is that it's actually easier and cheaper to do it this way. Studio One at Television Centre (universally known as TC1) is the best-equipped studio in the country, and *Strictly Come Dancing* – a live-music-and-performance show with complex lights and a real-time voting component – demands all the resources that the modern TV producer has at their disposal. Of course, it would be impossible to book TC1 for the entire eight-week run as it's also home to a lot of other regular BBC shows, including *Blue Peter* and *Top of the Pops*, plus occasional specials like *Children in Need* and *Sports Personality of the Year*. To run the show from a smaller, less well-equipped studio would bring its own headaches – not least

necessitating a far greater reliance on hired equipment, which is extremely expensive. The first series of *Strictly Come Dancing* came from the smaller TC4, and when the second series was commissioned the decision was taken to move the show to the larger, state-of-the-art studio space, from which there's been no turning back.

'There are cheaper spaces available,' says studio resources manager Simon Littler, whose job it is to oversee every aspect of the physical production of the weekly show, 'but they can work out to be a lot more expensive. You'd have to go outside the M25 to a studio like Pinewood or Shepperton – and then you'd have to hire lights for the entire duration of the run, you'd have to transport everyone to and from the studio, pay for accommodation and build all the travelling time into the schedule. It's just not worth it. If we're in TC1 everyone can get there easily, we only have to hire lights for three days a week, and we have everything we need right there.'

STRICTLY ON SCHEDULE

Working within this extraordinarily tight framework, the *Strictly Come Dancing* team has evolved a weekly timetable that sounds almost impossible to maintain, yet which has kept the show running without major

headaches for three series. In order to be ready for the live show on Saturday, they need to get into TC1 on Wednesday, as soon as the previous show moves out. The studio is basically a lightproof, soundproof box with a very flat floor, 10,500 square feet in size, and everything that you see on screen has to be put there deliberately. The first thing to go in is lighting, and

Saturday night, and the Strictly Come Dancing *set is reassembled, dressed, lit and ready for another show.*

Littler's team would start rigging overnight on Wednesday, into Thursday morning. There are 300 lighting hoists in TC1, including a lot of 'specials' – lights that move, project patterns or follow the dancers, which are programmed and remote-controlled from the director's gallery – all of which have to be installed and wired up before anything else can be done. Some of the lights live in Television Centre, but several have to be hired in specially, and they arrive on 40-foot trucks, which have to be unloaded into the studio in the small hours of Thursday morning.

By 6 a.m. on Thursday all the lighting should be in place, every light plugged into the control board and ready to be programmed by the lighting designer. That's when the scenic team takes over and starts building (or, rather, rebuilding) the familiar dance palace that forms the set of *Strictly Come Dancing*. They start off with the large mezzanine area behind the drapes and the stairs – from where we see the presenters appearing at the beginning of every show, and where the dancers are interviewed after their performances. The rest of the set is built around that: the stairs, the bandstand, the dance floor and the judges' area. Some of the pieces, such as the sweeping staircase, are very big and can simply be wheeled into TC1 and bolted onto the mezzanine. Others, such as the flying arches, are smaller and more fiddly, and have to be more or less rebuilt after every show.

The most complicated piece of the set is also the most important: the dance floor. Specially designed by *Strictly Come Dancing*'s set designer Patrick Doherty, it consists of a metal framework that sits on a layer of foam on the studio's concrete floor (which has to be freshly painted every week), topped off with a cladding of plywood and a parquet surface. It has to be bouncy enough to give the dancers' legs the kind of shock absorption that they need, but it also has to be thin and light enough to be transported and stored in between shows. The secret of the *Strictly Come Dancing* floor is that it comes to pieces – about 20 individual bits (large enough that they can be comfortably carried by two men) that are brought into the studio and put together like a giant jigsaw for every show.

Once the floor is in place, the audience areas are built on decking that sits on the studio floor, and then, while the carpenters and painters are putting the finishing touches to the joins and edges of the set, the electricians arrive to install the hundreds of little colour-changing LEDs that deck the staircase and arches. 'We've made a time-lapse film of the set being put together,' says Simon Littler, 'and it's amazing to watch. There are hundreds of people involved every single time we do it; it's slow and labour-intensive but it works.'

By Friday afternoon, all the hard work has paid off, and the studio is ready for the first camera rehearsal. 'That's the deadline that we're all aiming for. In theory, every tablecloth is in place, every bit of carpet nailed down before the cameras start working. It sounds impossible, but we've had plenty of practice now, so generally speaking it's all there on time.'

The camera rehearsal involves the dancers going through their paces on the floor, making sure that everything's ready for the live show on Saturday. 'Everything has to be in place,' says Littler, 'because it's live television. If something goes wrong, you can't go for a retake. We have to have systems in place that cover every eventuality – that's why it's such a long set-up. People sometimes ask me why I have such a big team of

Blackpool

At least once during series one and two, *Strictly Come Dancing* decamped for a live show to the Tower Ballroom, Blackpool – the spiritual home of ballroom dancing. 'We usually had to go because there was a big event pre-booked into TC1,' says Littler, 'but it became a great tradition on the show. The challenges at Blackpool are very different. Obviously we had a ready-made set, and it's the most wonderful interior – but it's not fitted up for live

broadcasts at all. We had to run miles of cables into the

theatre from a generator, going through the doors and windows and over the theatre balcony. Then we had to build cages to protect all the outside-broadcast equipment; Blackpool is a pretty lively place on a Saturday night, and if we hadn't fenced all our stuff into a pound it would have just got destroyed. We even had to get police and local-authority permission to remove benches from the pedestrian area outside the theatre so that we could park our trucks. It was a huge operation, and those were very, very late nights.'

people in the studio who don't seem to be doing very much a lot of the time. The truth is that for every bit of kit that could possibly go wrong you have to have someone keeping an eye out. It's a bit like building a house of cards in a hurricane: it only works if you have one person to hold every single card in place.'

THE SHOW GOES ON

After all the preparation, the *Strictly Come Dancing* set is only in place for a few hours. The band comes in on Saturday morning for its soundcheck, the presenters and dancers come out of make-up and then, on

As you'll never see it: technical operations carry on right up until the last moment before the show starts.

Saturday afternoon, everyone is ready for the dress rehearsal. After that, the audience is allowed into the studio, and the show is on.

While the programme is on air, most of the behind-the-scenes team members are sitting up in the gallery, making sure that everything is going according to plan. Littler's job is to keep an eye on everything that's going on – fire-fighting problems as they turn up and, crucially, making sure that the

Production facts

As if learning to dance wasn't hard enough, here are some facts and figures from behind the scenes in series three.

- Over the course of the series, contestants danced for 2554 hours, or 106 days, or 15.2 weeks
- They clocked up 2128 miles between them
- One set of false eyelashes does one girl for two shows; the make-up department used 38 sets
- One bottle of fake tan is enough for one couple; 75 bottles were used over the course of the series
- 3.4 litres of hairspray were used
- The costume department had to create 200 individual outfits
- 2.3 million crystals have been sewn on to outfits
- 855 metres of fabric have gone into making dresses
- 2760 hours spent making dresses
- Viewing figures for series three peaked for the final, which was watched by 10, 400,000 people – a whopping 42% audience share. Ten million also tuned into the results show
- The final of the last American series in February 2006 attracted over 27 million viewers
- Total number of votes cast in series three: 12,340,088 (nearly 5 million of which were for the final)
- Total number of votes cast over three series tops 14 million
- Series three raised over £1.5 million for *Children in Need*
- All three series have raised a total of over £3 million for *Children in Need* and *Comic Relief*

live feed is being picked up by both BBC1 and BBC3. 'If the feed does go down,' Littler says, 'there's a reserve in place, and that's my call. We can never allow ourselves to risk just having blank screens.'

But it's not all high-tech. 'We actually spend a lot of time in the gallery adding up the judges' scores in our heads. We could have given them fancy voting equipment that added up the scores automatically, but Karen [Smith] decided from the word go that the judges really had to have paddles with numbers on that they would hold up. The floor manager sneaks in to see the judges a few seconds before they announce their scores, they tell him what they're going to award, and he jumps out of shot to radio the scores up to Karen and me. So we stand around going, "Eight… six… that's 14… plus six is 20, plus seven… 27! 27!", checking each other's mental arithmetic.'

Fortunately, the system changed in the third series, when the judges were equipped with individual keypads that flashed the scores straight down to the gallery – and even added up the totals, thus taking one small but vital task off the producers' shoulders.

The Way You Look Tonight

While the dancers are busy in the studio mastering the footwork that will, they hope, lead them to glory, there's a huge team of hair and make-up artists, costume designers and stylists preparing the elaborate, often expensive outfits that will help all the contestants to make an impact on judges and audiences. As much as it's a dance show, Strictly Come Dancing has also become a byword for glamour – and each and every look that twirls across the floor is the result of weeks, sometimes months, of preparation.

It starts with the costumes – and these aren't just pretty off-the-peg dresses and suits that you might wear to a party. Dance clothes are complicated bits of technical kit that have to look good (and not rip!) while the wearer puts them through the most demanding of workouts. 'If you just wore normal clothes for *Strictly Come Dancing*, you'd be in big trouble,' says Su Judd, costume stylist for the show. 'The men have special dance trousers made of a high-grade stretch polyester, cut very wide in the crotch and with a very high waist – otherwise the shirt would come out, and the trousers would split at the seams. Even with the specialist dance trousers, we do have the odd accident – so the men wear black underpants, just in case. We don't want to see any flashes of white! The trousers are long in the leg too,

so that we don't see socks or bare legs. The jackets are amazing: the shoulders are made so that even when the arms are up in the air, they look flat – ordinarily you'd get a lump – and the arms are extra-long so they don't ride up. There isn't actually a waistcoat; the bit at the front is just holding everything in place.

'The women's costumes are even more specialized. All those dresses that you see are basically built round a made-to-measure leotard that the dancer just steps into. Some of them have zips, but most of them are just lycra with the rest of the dress attached over it. The leotard is always made in the same colour as the dress, so you won't notice it

when the dress moves. The leotards stretch every which way, they move with you as you dance and they support you in all the right places. If you wore a normal dress and you were thrown back in a Tango, for instance, your chest would fall out. These hold you in, nice and firm!'

Su Judd's job as costume stylist is to bring all the different clothing elements together – and then persuade the contestants to wear them! 'I work closely with the designers and makers of the clothes, but to be honest the major part of my job is convincing the celebrities to dress the part, and to reassure them that they're going to look great. I know all the rules – I can do the Trinny and Susannah thing – so they trust me to a certain extent. Whatever size or shape they are, whether they've got a big bust or short legs, I'm going to make them look good. But this isn't just fashion styling, this is getting people

into clothes that feel and look very unusual, and they don't necessarily have the confidence to put them on. The professional dancers are used to wearing this gear in their working lives, but for the celebrities it's a big leap of faith, and they're terrified of looking stupid. It was particularly difficult with the first series of *Strictly Come Dancing*: nobody knew if it was going to be a hit or not, and they didn't want to make fools of themselves. It's easier now we've done three very successful series, I must say!'

Some stars are easier to dress than others. 'Believe it or not,' says Judd, 'the person we had the biggest problem with in the first series was Natasha Kaplinsky. She would be the first to admit that she had serious misgivings about the show. She's a newsreader, a serious journalist in a predominantly male world, and she did not want to blow her credibility by coming out looking like a fruit salad. When we first met, I took along a drawing that the designers had done, and a selection of beautiful fabrics; we sat down in her dressing room at the BBC and she just burst into tears, "I can't do it, I can't do it!" I really thought we were going to lose her at that stage – which would have been such a shame, because she's got such a great figure we couldn't wait to start dressing her. I knew she'd look good even in the most extreme outfits – and dance costumes are pretty full-on – but she was terrified. So I talked to her about the kind of clothes she likes to wear, and we went right back to very simple, safe looks to build up her confidence at the start of the show. Then it was just a question of working with her to achieve something we were both happy with.

'The fittings started out with Natasha wearing things that covered her from top to toe – then we'd get a pair of scissors and start cutting off a bit here, a bit there – literally while she's wearing it. Natasha hasn't got much chest, she's tall and elegant, so she's crying out for plunge necks and high splits – but that took some work. Brendan [Cole, Kaplinsky's dance partner] would be there supervising – the men can be very controlling about what the women wear, but I didn't mind in Brendan's case because he does have a good eye. Every week, we managed to get Natasha to wear a little less and show a little more. The breakthrough came in the fourth week, when we went to Blackpool and she was dancing the Jive. The dress was black, with cobalt-blue shoes, fringing at the hem and stones down the tights. The key to the Jive is seeing the legwork, so when we were fitting it, we cut the skirt really high. Natasha was desperately worried, but we knew it looked good, and Brendan was confident that she could do the dance properly. She nearly refused to go out in it, but by that time it was too late, the dress was made and everyone thought she looked great. We persuaded her at the eleventh hour, she went out and she did really well. For the first time, we realized that she was enjoying herself. After that, she was much more relaxed about what she'd wear. Mind you, we had taken along a bit of extra fringing so that we could lower the skirt, just in case she really wouldn't wear it – but she didn't need to know that! In the next few weeks, she just took flight. Her confidence was reflected in the clothes that she wore.'

CREATING THE DESIGNS

Outfits for the celebrities have to be designed well in advance, as making and fitting them is a costly process. For the women's dresses, the show employs Chrisanne Limited, the UK's leading dancewear makers. 'All the designers and makers at Chrisanne are ex-dancers,' says Judd, 'so they know exactly

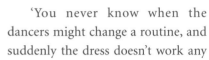

what will work. I go along for a consultation and we pick out colours and fabrics for the whole show, based on what's fashionable that season. Then they design the dresses for all the celebrities in all the dances. Those drawings go back to the female celebrities, they pick out the ones they like and they're sent back to Chrisanne to be redrawn. Once everyone's happy with the design and the colours, they make the dresses up. They're expensive: each dress costs anything from £1500 to £2500 apiece and is worn only once before being sold on.

Because *Strictly Come Dancing* is a live show with a competitive element, nobody quite knows from week to week what's going to be required on the night. Chrisanne's designs may have to be abandoned or completely reworked according to the dancers' needs – and that's no small undertaking when the garments are so intricate. The finishing touches of sparkle are all applied by hand just before the dress is worn. Chrisanne sends the dresses out to a group of specialists who hand-glue every single stone to the fabric – and that can be thousands of stones on a single dress. But even with such attention to detail, the best-laid plans can always go awry.

'You never know when the dancers might change a routine, and suddenly the dress doesn't work any more,' says Judd. 'I got a call in series two from Brendan Cole and Sarah Manners. She'd had a beautiful gold-and-turquoise dress designed for their Paso Doble, it was agreed on and half made, and then on the Sunday night I found a message at home saying. "Please don't be angry, but we've changed the routine." They'd decided to dance to 'Bring Me to Life' by Evanescence, which is quite a dark, gothic song, and they wanted to do a sort of Dracula routine. Well, gold and turquoise wasn't going to work for that! I put a stop on that dress, then grabbed a black outfit that Hanna had worn in a demonstration dance and just cut it in half, pinned bits in, draped a bit of fabric over Sarah's bum, stuck stones over the joins. Brendan just wore black trousers and a black bolero jacket, bare-chested. And it worked! But that's a very rare occurrence, I'd like to point out, just in case the dancers are reading this.'

Other factors can demand quick thinking in the costume department, such as rapid weight loss. something that affected quite a few of the celebrities as they

went through intense training. Both Aled Jones and James Martin lost considerable amounts of weight during training, which meant trousers had to be taken in and shirts bought in smaller sizes. But the biggest challenge came from Lesley Garrett, who lost 16lb in the first series – and totally changed shape as a result. 'She had to be refitted every week. Those dance leotards that the women wear are made to measure – they have to be a perfect fit, otherwise things will fall out – and Lesley's bum and bosom kept shrinking and shrinking. In the first show, she was worried about looking mumsy, and we'd done a lot of work on the dresses to make sure that she didn't look top heavy. There's no underwiring in a leotard, they hold your boobs in by squashing them, basically – so we had to devise something that would give Lesley adequate support while not letting her pop out in the middle of a dance. Then the weight started to come off, and we were remaking and refitting every single week. She was so pleased with her black and white Foxtrot dress that she bought it from us, and she wears it in her own stage show now.'

The men's outfits are far less labour-intensive than the women's – but there are

still plenty of challenges for Su Judd and her team. 'Men are, generally speaking, very conservative about what they're prepared to wear. They don't want to look camp. When Darren Gough turned up for the first photoshoot of series three, which is when I first met him, he was wearing a hoodie top with a jacket over it, and white trainers. He said, "This is how I want to look", and when he first saw the dance shoes he just said, "No way!". We even tried to find him trainers that he could dance in, because he wanted to keep a street image, but the producer wasn't having it, and he went into ballroom shoes. After three weeks, he wouldn't be parted from those shoes. By the time he did the Paso Doble, halfway through the series, he was starting to wear sparkly stones and net sleeves. You look at his Latin outfits throughout the competition, and you'll see a definite progression towards colour and glamour. Mind you, he had Lilia Kopylova pushing him all the way, and she has very definite ideas about what looks right. I don't think he really had that much choice!'

One person who didn't need much persuading to glam it up was Julian Clary. 'During his career, he's

worn just about everything. I actually had to tone him down. I didn't want him going out there looking bizarre; the men in the dance world consider themselves butch and manly, and they wouldn't be happy if they thought that Julian was sending them up. Fortunately, Julian is very fit and elegant, and it didn't take much to send him out looking like Fred Astaire. He looks good in suits. He always wanted a bit of sparkle, but it was restrained; it was very important that he didn't overshadow Erin. I liked him best in the more conservative outfits, the midnight-blue suits with a few stones. He looked very Hollywood.'

PREPARING FOR THE SHOW

Su Judd's team of eight dressers, plus assistants and designers from Chrisanne, has a huge job on the day of the live show. 'Every pair of dancers has a dresser assigned to them, plus we have Bruce and Tess, the band, the singers and the judges to take care of. I go into the studio on Friday and make sure everything is in place – from the clothes right down to the last bit of feather or trim – so when we start dressing them on Saturday there are no last-minute surprises. We let them see the clothes when they're rehearsing, but they can't dance in them, because they're so easily stained or ripped. After morning rehearsal they have lunch, then we dress them in time for the full dress rehearsal in the afternoon. I sit up in the control room, watching it on the monitors so that I can be certain it looks good on TV – there's still time to make any last tweaks, or repair things that get damaged. One week, Diarmuid stood on Nicole's skirt and ripped the fringe off; that was sewn back on in the nick of time.'

During the live broadcast, and in the period before the later results show, the contestants stay in their costumes but are encouraged to keep away from food and drink. 'I try to put capes over them, in case they drop something, and I ask them not to

dance, because we don't want any accidents. We spend a lot of that time in between the shows making small adjustments, telling them they were fantastic, basically keeping everyone in good spirits. We're not just dressers, you know. Half the time we're psychiatrists as well.'

FINISHING TOUCHES

When the clothes are on, the dances rehearsed, the band ready to strike up and the lights in position, the very last piece of the puzzle to be fitted into place is the hair and make-up. Make-up designer Sarah Burrows will be heading the series-four team. Here, Gilly Popham, make-up and hair designer for series one to three, tells us how it all works. 'It may come last but,' she says, 'it's often the first thing to be noticed. When the dancers step out onto the floor, people instantly take in the way they look – and that means the face and the head first. If that doesn't make a good impression, it can let everything else down, the costume, the dancing, the whole show.'

Erin Boag, Lilia Kopylova, Darren Bennett and Anton du Beke get ready for our photoshoot, with hairdressers Anna Winterburn and Brendon Midson, and make-up artists Jo Jenkins and Christine Bateman.

Hair and make-up can make or break a routine, and it's vital that they should not only fit in with the style of the dance but suit each individual as well. 'Some of them are willing to put themselves entirely into our hands,' says Popham. 'Denise Lewis, for instance, would let us do crazy things with her hair, putting in extensions, getting her to wear wigs and jewels. But some of them have a very particular look that they're unwilling to depart from. That can be difficult when you're trying to get them ready to get out and do a certain type of dance.'

The style that Popham and her team of artists employed on *Strictly Come Dancing* was, she says, 'traditional dance make-up modified for television. You can't go for the usual dance make-up – it's far

too strong. It's designed to be seen from the back row of an auditorium, so you have great thick lines around the eyes, the hair practically glued to the head. But on *Strictly Come Dancing*, these people are going to appear on screen in single close-ups, and we're going to see them backstage being interviewed. We can't send them out there looking like freaks. That was one of the problems with the old *Come Dancing* series: they didn't adapt the make-up enough, so the dancers looked like really strange mannequins. We toned the look down so it was closer to fashion make-up than stage – but it still has to look suitably dramatic. It's a very fine balance.'

Hair and make-up has to work with every other element of the performance, co-ordinating and emphasising elements present in the music, the choreography, the costume and the lighting. 'The first thing I did was talk to the producer about the overall look of the show, the sets, the lighting and the clothes, so that we were all aiming for the same style. In the first series, we went for a very high-fashion, glam look, which was reflected in the make-up. The second series was a bit more elegant, more Hollywood, with period elements from the 20s through to the 50s. There's always a guiding principle to what we do, and it's the finishing touches like the colour of nails or the use of hair ornaments that really set the tone.'

Getting the show ready is a massive task: it wasn't unusual for Popham and her team to have 40 people to prepare. It's not just the dancers – there are the presenters, the judges, the singers and the guest artists as well. 'We got in at nine in the morning, and we worked non-stop into the night. We got a 20-minute break if we were lucky. The team that I had working for me were all top stylists, who saw this as a great challenge.'

The team meets half an hour before they start work to check through the programme for the day; the hair and make-up designer issues them with a call sheet that details every single make-up and hair look that they need to create. 'Then we get cracking. First of all we do their hair – and it's not unusual to be sewing in hairpieces or switches, which takes a lot of time. They have to be very firmly fixed – you can't have false hair flying off in the middle of a dance – but it also has to move naturally on camera, so we can't glue it down. After that we just work our way through everyone. The contestants can be in make-up for up to two and half hours. It's not like going out for the night; we do

Julian Clary was only too happy to look the part, and Erin was brave enough to allow him to practise his make-up skills, as well as his dancing skills, on her!

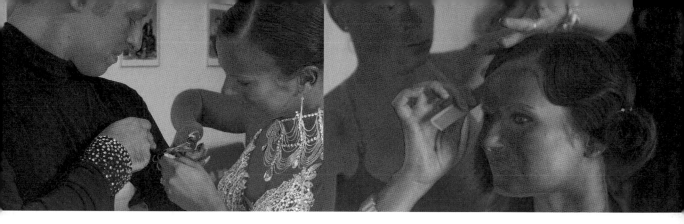

absolutely everything. We paint their nails, sometimes we do false nails, there are false eyelashes to stick on, sometimes there's fake tan to apply. And the men aren't any easier – there's a lot of general grooming that you have to do on a man. Shaving the back of the neck so it looks tidy, trimming the hair, the eyebrows, the facial hair, nose, ears, the lot. If they're baring their chest or arms we have to make them look good; I spent hours putting cream on Martin Offiah's body so that he went out shining. In the first series, we used a lot of that – the shiny look was very fashionable at the time, to the extent that some people looked as if they'd been dipped in a vat of Vaseline.'

Popham's job didn't end when the show started either; there was always something to be done. 'We were the first people the dancers saw when they arrived in the morning, and were the last ones they had contact with before they'd go on stage. We'd be there with them in the wings, powdering them, touching up lips, boosting their confidence. They have to feel that they look fantastic before they go on, and so that was our job too.'

The professional dancers are used to wearing full warpaint and going out in front of an audience, but for some of the celebrity contestants it's a new and unnerving experience. 'Even the actors and entertainers find it weird,' says Popham, 'because they're not going out there to do their usual job. They're appearing as themselves, so they want to look good, but they're doing something that they're not used to doing. The make-up is a mask to some extent, giving them confidence. But it could be very difficult to persuade them to take on the look we think they need.'

Just as Su Judd spends her time talking celebrities into showing more skin, Gilly Popham had to persuade the artists to adopt looks they wouldn't normally be seen dead in. 'Some of them were very open to change, but others had a fixed idea of how they should look, and were not happy for us to mess around with that. It's part of their armour. Esther Rantzen, for instance, had a very definite idea of her own image, and when we first met she told me, "I will not wear false nails, false eyelashes or red lipstick." By the time the series was over, she was wearing the lot and she loved it. I think *Strictly Come Dancing* gave her a new idea of herself; she's a very attractive woman with a great face and a fantastic figure, and that really came across in the show. The turning point came when I wanted to get her into a red wig for her Tango. She found one that she really liked, but it was far too expensive – I only had a small budget for hairpieces, and this would have really dented it. So Esther went and bought it herself, and she looked great in it. After she'd been knocked out of the show, she had her hair cut and coloured in the same style as the wig!'

Not everyone is quite so eager to embrace a personal transformation. In the third series, Gloria Hunniford was afraid of having an 'inappropriate' style foisted on her, and took great care to develop a look that she felt comfortable in. She was very particular about appearing elegant and respectable in restrained styles that were appropriate to her age. It was a shame in some ways, because she's a gorgeous woman and we could have put her into some knock-out stuff. She relaxed after a while though – and the Jive jacket she wore came from her own wardrobe, with stones added by us – but she never really let go. By contrast, Patsy Palmer and Zoe Ball went with the glamour from the word go, and embraced it fully. Zoe totally changed her look, rediscovered her femininity, stopped wearing black all the time and now appears in public wearing gowns in bright colours.'

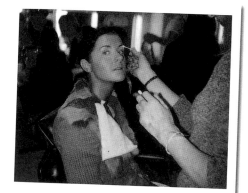

Strictly Come Dancing has a high-gloss style that's integral to the show's success, and that means that the hair and make-up team is never off duty. 'We were on our feet all day,' says Gilly Popham. 'At the start of the series we were sweet-talking people into trying new looks; at the end of the series, we were doing changes for them so that they could do two dances in a show. And there was endless maintenance; we had to get onto the floor when we could to touch up the presenters and judges. That's risky. Once a couple of make-up artists got caught on camera trying to powder the judges – they get so hot sitting under the lights. Tess Daly covered it brilliantly – she said, "There are two mad fans trying to nobble the judges!" – but we had to be extra-careful that we didn't get spotted.'

At the end of the night, when the final dance has been danced and the results announced, the make-up team is on hand to help clean up the performers. They take out all the hair ornaments and pieces – they can't have them ripped out any-old-how – but the rest is up to them. They get a bag of cleansing products, and the team leave them to it.

‘At the end of the night, when the final dance has been danced and the final score announced, the make-up team is on call again to get the performers cleaned up and ready for bed’

Lets Face the Music

One of the hardest – and most expensive – decisions that faced the producers of Strictly Come Dancing *concerned music. Would they use recorded music – familiar to audiences and competitors, but completely dead in terms of entertainment – or would they go to the trouble and cost of hiring a live band? 'There was never any doubt in my mind,' says Creative Head of Format Entertainment Karen Smith. 'It had to be live. All the great entertainment shows have had a live band. and I wanted to capture that feeling of an old-fashioned dance hall, where a couple would go to hear a proper band. If we were going to appeal to a big audience, and give that feeling of genuine entertainment, it was vital to get the best in the business.'*

A new musical director, David Arch, is in charge of the music for series four. David Arch is a writer, arranger and musician and a well-known face on the band circuit. He has worked with everyone from Westlife to Alanis Morisette, and has arranged music for box office hits like Notting Hill and Chocolat. Here, musical director for series one to three, Laurie Holloway, tells us how it all works. Holloway put together a big band – three trumpets, three trombones, four woodwind, piano, guitar, bass, drums and percussion, recruited a team of singers and awaited orders. He knew that he was going to have to produce eight to ten songs per show, and he knew that most of that music would be new arrangements of contemporary popular songs. The rest he had to work out as he went along.

'For that first series, I wrote every crotchet and quaver that was played,' he says. 'For three months I didn't leave my music room, I was just writing, writing, writing. I became a zombie, and the worst thing is, I enjoyed it and I got totally hooked on the deadlines. But, for the second series, I had to call in a bit of help – the series got longer, and there's only so much that one person can do.'

MAKING THE MUSIC

The process of turning pop songs into live dance music calls on a wide range of skills, and also takes full advantage of new technology. The songs are chosen by the production team, 'with a little bit of advice from me,' says Holloway, 'because at first they didn't understand basic things about tempo. They'd send me songs for Waltzes that weren't in 3:4 time, and I'd have to explain that while I could work a lot of miracles, that was one that was beyond me.' The selections mixed classics ('The Lady Is a Tramp', 'Let's Face the Music and Dance') with pop standards ('Roxanne', 'How Deep Is Your Love') and more recent chart material ('Leave Right Now', 'Livin' La Vida Loca').

It was one thing for Holloway to rearrange the songs for his band ('That's the sort of thing I can pretty much do with my eyes closed'), but first the numbers have to be edited to fit the one-minute-30-second format of the routines. So the commercial tracks were emailed to studio wizard Graham Jarvis, who, in consultation with the dancers, picked out the highlights of a song and glues them together into a working track. 'I used software called Cubase SX,' says Jarvis. 'It's very good for cutting and pasting, but it also allowed me to smooth out the tempos and add false

endings where necessary. Older songs tend to vary a lot in tempo – they speed up for the chorus or the final verse – and that's hard for the dancers. Also, a lot of commercial tracks fade at the end, and the dancers need a definite ending. I could sort all that out in the studio, and provide an edited track that they would rehearse to.'

Jarvis's edited version was then emailed to Laurie Holloway, who played it on his computer and started arranging. 'Computers are wonderful things,' he says, 'because they've cut out all that toing and

froing we used to do. In the old days, I had to meet my music copyist in a lay-by on the M4 to hand things over; now I just wait for it to drop into my mailbox. But when it comes to arranging, I do it with paper and pencil – it's what I'm used to, and it's faster.

'So I listened to Graham's track, then went to the piano and worked out the key. I marked up my scoresheets, then wrote down the intro and all the different band parts. I had to transpose some parts onto other instruments – I don't have strings in my band, for instance, so I might give the string part to flutes, or I could do them on my keyboard, a Yamaha Clavinova. The whole thing took me about three hours, then I faxed it all over to my music copyist who produced the band parts. It was a pretty slick operation.'

While the musical director is busy with the arrangements, the dancers are rehearsing to the edited studio track – so there can be an element of surprise when they first hear the live version. 'It shouldn't be too much of a shock,' says Holloway, 'because we observe strict tempo, and all the bits that they're used to will be there. Once or twice I've had dancers (naming no names) going off at me about how I ruined their chances by changing the music, but I check back and make sure that our arrangements are identical in all fundamental respects to what they've used. It sounds different – it's a live band – but it's the same piece.'

PLAYING IT LIVE

On the day of the show, the band has only an hour's rehearsal time for all its numbers, and 20 minutes of that is taken up with sound-checks. 'All we could do is run through our parts and make sure the numbers work. To all intents and purposes, the musicians were sight-reading. But that's not a problem, that's what they're trained to do – they're the best session musicians in the country. The A-team. And if any of

them weren't available, there'd be another A-team. There was no such thing as a B-team.' After the band rehearsal (which the dancers often spy on, to get a sneak preview of the sound), there is a full dress run – the first time that all the elements of the show come together. And then, show time.

'The best thing about *Strictly Come Dancing*,' says Holloway, 'is that it's live. There are no retakes. It's like old-fashioned light entertainment, but it has much more atmosphere. It takes me back to the days when I used to play for the *Rolf Harris Show,* or the *Val Doonican Show.* I like that big-band feel, and it's something new for me.'

The success of *Strictly Come Dancing* has led to more big-band gigs for Holloway and his team – 'which is great, but a lot of hard work. I always had a trio before, and, believe me, that's a lot easier to manage.' He's also become firm friends with his presenter-in-chief. 'Bruce is a jazz piano player, too, so we have a bit of fun writing things together. He lives

In the spirit of Saturday-night live entertainment the programme's band often made way for some of the music industry's star talents to join in. Guest artists have included Donny Osmond, Westlife, Michelle Williams (from Destiny's Child) and Shania Twain.

just a few miles from my house, so it's easy to get together and play.'

When he wasn't putting the dancers through their paces, Holloway was at ITV providing music for Michael Parkinson's show. 'That runs from September too, so during the autumn I'd be working flat out. Parkinson is two days a week; *Strictly Come Dancing* is five. It's great for my ego, but it didn't doing a lot for my social life.'

And the secret of his success? 'I work fast,' says Holloway, 'and I don't make mistakes. But to be honest, I think the reason producers like me is because I turn up on time and I don't get drunk till after the show's over. You know what musicians can be like.'

Series One

David Dickinson

He knows his way around a piece of antique mahogany, but could bargain-king David Dickinson cut it on the dance floor? And how far would his cult following take him when the competition got tough?

NAME David Dickinson
DAY JOB TV presenter, antiques expert
DANCE PARTNER Camilla Dallerup
BEST DANCE The Quickstep in week two, to 'Let's Face the Music and Dance'. 'You took off!' said Bruno, not the hardest man to please.
WORST DANCE The Cha Cha Cha in week one. Despite an impressive sparkly outfit, Dickinson looked ill at ease and unfit, and only scored 16.
THE JUDGES SAID Len: 'You're a marvellous sport, but you're too nice a guy for the Tango.'
HOW DID THEY DO? Knocked out after three weeks.

As the senior contestant in the first series, David Dickinson was brought into the mix to appeal to older viewers – but, as canny Creative Head of Format Entertainment Karen Smith was well aware, his audience stretched right through to students and children, thanks to his catchphrase-heavy performance on *Bargain Hunt*. During the training there was much speculation as to whether he would prove to be a 'bobby-dazzler' or simply 'cheap as chips', but the laughs started to wear off when he threw himself into training with Camilla Dallerup. It soon became clear that Dickinson, for all his worldly charm, wasn't a dance natural; in fact, he seemed almost entirely lacking a sense of rhythm.

Then the Dickinson–Dallerup dance-floor début made an unforgettable impact. Bruce Forsyth had given him a big build-up as they'd chosen the song 'Sex Bomb' for their inaugural Cha Cha Cha. While Dallerup tried to hold the judges' eyes, Dickinson walked around the floor waggling his hands and visibly counting the beats. The judges were less than impressed. 'It's all pomp and no circumstance,' said Arlene Phillips, to which Dickinson offered a tart rejoinder: 'At 62, I try my best, love.' He clearly wasn't pleased with the harsh verdict, but returned after a week of intensive training to execute a creditable Quickstep. The scores reflected the improvement, but it wasn't enough to save them, and Dickinson was knocked out in the third week.

Lesley Garrett

If they awarded points for enthusiasm, Lesley Garrett would have won the first series hands down. No other dancer threw herself into the show with such gusto, or enjoyed it so much – but that wasn't always enough to impress the judges.

Public performance held no fear for Lesley Garrett, whose operatic career has taken her to audiences all over the world. But dancing isn't quite the same, as she was the first to admit. Partner Anton du Beke provided the necessary inspiration, and as the training progressed Garrett found her wings. 'No matter how hectic my day is, I come here and my spirit soars,' she said, and didn't even complain when du Beke fell, hard, on top of her during rehearsal.

Garrett's dance-floor début surprised even her. In a figure-hugging mauve dress, with her hair up, she glided through a Waltz to 'He Was Beautiful', and she was so excited when she completed a successful first round that she let out an ear-splitting soprano shriek. 'That was the most exciting moment of my whole life,' she told Tess Daly backstage, visibly shaking to prove it. They ended the first show with the best scores from the judges and looked like favourites to win.

As the weeks went on, the pounds fell off; Garrett had to attend constant costume refittings as her body shape changed. Her dancing improved too, and in the third week she and du Beke fought heavy colds to deliver a very respectable Rumba. Their scores kept high, audiences liked them, but cracks began to appear in the sixth week when she admitted she was 'tetchy and cross', finding it hard to learn the Foxtrot. The judges liked what she did and they worked hard but, in a controversial decision, they were knocked out in the seventh week when viewers saved Christopher Parker for the final. Garrett was in tears, but quickly rallied her spirits. 'I think every woman on the planet should have half an hour with Anton du Beke,' she enthused.

NAME Lesley Garrett, CBE
DAY JOB Opera singer
DANCE PARTNER Anton du Beke
BEST DANCE Best and worst came in the same week. The Foxtrot in week six earned 34 points, inspiring Bruno Tonioli to call her 'a class act'.
WORST DANCE Later in the same show, the Cha Cha Cha to Kylie Minogue's 'Spinning Around' let her down. She started off on the wrong foot, and never really recovered.
THE JUDGES SAID Arlene: 'You have a dancer inside of you, and I'd like to see it come out.'
HOW DID THEY DO? Third place, knocked out after the seventh show.

Verona Joseph

Strictly Come Dancing proved an uphill struggle for actor Verona Joseph, who was not only filming all day but trying to move house as well.

NAME Verona Joseph
DAY JOB Actor, plays Jess Griffin in *Holby City*
DANCE PARTNER Paul Killick
BEST DANCE Weirdly, Joseph got the best marks for the dance that broke the rules, the Cha Cha Cha in the first week.
WORST DANCE Their remaining three dances all scored a respectable 24, but marks could have been higher if they'd stayed within the rule book.
THE JUDGES SAID Bruno: 'Buckets of sex appeal.' Len: 'All sizzle, no sausage.'
HOW DID THEY DO? Knocked out after the fourth show.

It was never going to be easy for Verona Joseph, who fitted the programme and training into her commitment to BBC1's war-horse, *Holby City*. Dance partner Paul Killick travelled to and from the BBC's Elstree Studios to rehearse with Joseph in her breaks – but the pressure was showing from the start, with the actor complaining of fainting fits and panic attacks. You'd never have known it, however, when they stepped out in the first show, she in a green spangled dress, he in a leopardskin jacket, to deliver a controversial Cha Cha Cha. Killick ended the dance by lifting his partner off the floor and spinning her around – which got the judges in a fury. 'You broke a rule!' shrieked Arlene, but the duo were unrepentant.

It was clear from the start that Joseph was a dance natural – and there were even mutterings from other dancers that she was professionally trained and so had an unfair advantage. 'My professional training to date was three weeks of ballet when I was seven, and four weeks of contemporary dance when I was 14,' she said. 'If that means I'm a professional dancer, then my mum got value for money, darling!'

But stress was getting the better of Joseph by the fourth week – not only was Killick proving to be a hard taskmaster but she was also in the throes of moving house. Their Paso Doble was done on a wing and a prayer and minimum rehearsal, and despite the fact that both of them looked hotter than hell on the dance floor, their scores crashed, and they were knocked out. Joseph seemed relieved. 'Now I can concentrate on moving,' she said. 'Paul deserved someone who could give him 100 per cent.'

Martin Offiah

He excels on the rugby field – but could Martin 'Chariots' Offiah cut it on the dance floor?

There was no doubt that Martin Offiah was fit – apart from a niggling old shoulder injury he was in full match form. But there's a big difference between the strength and stamina required for rugby, and the grace and co-ordination demanded by ballroom dancing. 'I've danced a bit in nightclubs,' said Offiah, 'but nothing with the discipline of ballroom.' As he trained with Erin Boag, he soon realized that dance was not a soft option – but it had compensations. 'I'd rather dance with a woman in a skimpy outfit than play rugby with a load of sweaty geezers,' he said.

Offiah's first outing with Erin was a Waltz, and he surprised everyone by getting through it with some style. He was far from relaxed, though, and the tension was written all over his face. Len Goodman was encouraging, but Arlene Phillips gave a double-edged compliment: 'For a rugby player, you dance very well.'

However, his confidence boosted, Offiah soon relaxed and as the weeks progressed his dancing – and his dress sense – improved. Sober suits went out, and revealing outfits appeared in various hot shades. Offiah's Jive in the third week got a standing ovation – and not just because he'd overcome an ankle injury to perform it. The newspapers started to buzz with some half-hearted rumours that Offiah and Boag were clicking off the dance floor as well as on, but Offiah quashed that talk: 'Erin is like Alex Ferguson to me. She's the toughest manager I've ever had. I nearly had a dance shoe in the head.'

Sadly, Offiah fell victim to the Parker Factor. As Chris Parker's popularity soared in inverse proportion to his dancing ability, Offiah was knocked out.

NAME Martin Offiah MBE
DAY JOB Wigan and England rugby player
DANCE PARTNER Erin Boag
BEST DANCE Best first for Offiah: his Waltz in the first show scored 25 from the judges.
WORST DANCE The Rumba in show two only scored 21 ('No hip action,' complained Craig), as did the Jive the following week ('Glued to the floor,' said Arlene).
THE JUDGES SAID Craig: 'You put your butt to much better use!' Arlene: 'Charming, but lazy legs.'
HOW DID THEY DO? Knocked out after the sixth show.

Natasha Kaplinsky

Although the most reluctant of contestants, Natasha Kaplinsky discovered a hidden talent for dance and enjoyed the experience so much, not only did she win – but also went on to co-present part of the next series.

NAME Natasha Kaplinsky
DAY JOB Presents BBC1's *Breakfast News*
DANCE PARTNER Brendan Cole
BEST DANCE Natasha and Brendan pulled out all the stops for the Samba in week five, and scored 37 – possibly inspired by the presence of Brendan's mother, visiting from New Zealand!
WORST DANCE Only 24 out of 40 for the week-three Jive, marked down for breaking the rules.
THE JUDGES SAID Arlene: 'Staggering! You are a professional dancer!' Len: 'If they don't win, it's a travesty.'
HOW DID THEY DO? Winner of series one; Kaplinsky liked it so much she co-presented part of series two!

Natasha Kaplinsky was not *Strictly Come Dancing*'s most eager recruit. 'I begged my bosses to ban me from doing the show,' she says. 'I'd worked so hard to build up credibility as a newsreader, a woman in a male-dominated world, and I thought this could throw it all away. At one point I was seriously considering "falling" off the kerb and twisting my ankle. But it didn't work – I ended up in training.'

Kaplinsky's is the most dramatic of all the transformations wrought by the show. Within weeks, she'd discovered a new confidence and dance ability that she never knew she had. 'It was by far the most frightening thing I've done in my life. I've presented some pretty big news stories, but nothing can compare with the terror of going out in front of millions of people to do something I didn't think I could do. But once I got dancing, and realized I could do it, my attitude changed. I'd only had two dance lessons in my life – but suddenly I was acquiring a new skill. Brendan [Cole] was a real perfectionist, but he knew when not to push me. It was as much about emotional coaching as physical training. The sense of achievement is like nothing else I've ever experienced.'

Kaplinsky was overwhelmed by the support of the voting public; but also found herself splashed all over the newspapers. 'I was shocked at the extent to which the papers started to write about me and the other contestants – I couldn't bear to think that people might believe the things that were being made up about me. But, to be honest, I was getting up at 3am, doing breakfast news, then rehearsing all day for Saturday; there wasn't time to get upset.'

Christopher Parker

The EastEnders pin-up proved that you don't have to be a great dancer to get the public vote – but would Christopher Parker be able to cope with the weekly grilling he got from the judges?

It didn't start well. Christopher Parker, idol of millions of teenage girls for his puppy-dog performance as Albert Square's Spencer Moon, was the first to admit that he had 'two left feet'. Even his *EastEnders* co-star Shane Richie urged him to 'Please walk away! You can't even walk in time!' Parker laughed off the criticism at first and threw himself into training with his partner, Hanna Karttunen, but It was apparent from the very first show that he was hampered by an almost total absence of aptitude. The pair's Cha Cha Cha, to 'Lady Marmalade', featured some fancy footwork from Karttunen, but not much from Parker.

The public took to Parker, and brought him back week after week ('He's like a boomerang!' said Bruce Forsyth), but the judges were a different matter, and soon their regular humiliation of Parker became one of the show's must-see moments. Parker didn't take it lying down. By the sixth week, he was fighting back. After a disastrous Paso Doble ('Paso dreadful, my darling!' wailed Bruno), which scored only 15 out of a possible 40, Parker was visibly upset. 'What do I have to do?' he pleaded. 'I'm trying my hardest!' Over the coming weeks his obvious, valiant efforts in rehearsal (not to mention his cute expressions of vulnerability and dismay) won the public's heart; Shane Richie started turning up to support his screen brother, and Parker made it into the final. But the judges were implacable, basing their scores not on Parker's lovable personality but on his dancing. Everyone hated them for it, and Parker crashed out of a final he never expected to reach.

NAME Christopher Parker
DAY JOB Actor
DANCE PARTNER Hanna Karttunen
BEST DANCE The Foxtrot in week four. 'Even Arlene was positive!' gasped a shocked Parker.
WORST DANCE The samba in week five, and the Paso Doble in week six, which prompted Bruno to say, 'You were stamping on cockroaches!'
THE JUDGES SAID 'If there were an award for bravery,' said Arlene, 'you'd win it.' Craig was less charitable, and repeatedly called Christopher 'naff'.
STICKY MOMENTS In their first dance, Parker tripped over and got headbutted by Karttunen.
HOW DID THEY DO? Runners-up of series one.

Claire Sweeney

Expectations were high when Claire Sweeney, star of stage musicals, hit the Strictly Come Dancing *studio. But would it go her way or would the judges mark her too hard?*

NAME Claire Sweeney
DAY JOB Actor and TV presenter who also starred in the West End production of *Chicago*
DANCE PARTNER John Byrnes
BEST DANCE The Tango in week three. Len described her as 'a panther stalking its prey'.
WORST DANCE The Rumba in week two, which still managed to score a respectable 26. Len accused them of hiding the steps under flashy effects.
THE JUDGES SAID Bruno dismissed their début Waltz as 'boring,' but after their Paso Doble he described Claire as 'quite the sexiest bull I've seen.'
HOW DID THEY DO? Knocked out in week five.

'I'm not a good dancer,' insisted Claire Sweeney during training, 'I'm just someone who can get away with it.' But anyone who had seen her gliding through the Waltz with professional partner John Byrnes would have found that hard to believe – and Sweeney had to battle with her enhanced reputation for the rest of the show. When the judges marked her harshly, Sweeney complained, 'I can only do my best! I'm not a trained dancer!' and she never really recovered from that initial disappointment.

That's not to say that she didn't give the show her best shot. In fact, Sweeney and Byrnes stayed high in the ranking throughout their five weeks on the show, but in the end they failed to win enough public sympathy to keep them in the competition. In the third week, their fiery Tango inspired the judges to get out their '9' paddles for the first time in the competition, and they ended the show at the top of the table, well ahead of their nearest rivals, Lesley and Anton.

But, at the end of week five, the viewers decided to vote them off. 'I feel disappointed, obviously,' said Sweeney after the shock result came through. 'I really enjoyed tonight; it was the first time it didn't feel like a competition. Maybe I was having too much fun.' She'd realized – too late in the event – that the key to *Strictly Come Dancing* success wasn't just fancy footwork, but audience sympathy. 'We had a plan if we got through this week,' she said. 'I was going to get myself photographed with a plaster cast on one of my legs.'

Jason Wood

Unknown to prime-time audiences, would Jason Wood prove to be the unexpected hit of the series? Only if he could learn to dance well enough to impress the judges…

It seemed like a marriage made in heaven: Jason Wood, the critically lauded stand-up comedian, and world dance champion Kylie Jones. Kylie and Jason; it had worked before, so why not for *Strictly Come Dancing*? But it soon became clear that Wood wasn't working, either for the judges or the audiences. He seemed nervous from the start, unsure whether to send up the whole thing as a camp joke, or to knuckle down and concentrate on the dancing. It didn't help that there was over 12 inches difference in their heights; 'It's like Beauty and the Beast,' said Wood during training. 'Maybe being so abnormal we might just win some hearts.'

They took to the studio floor in the first week with a Waltz – the most elegant of dances – but Wood couldn't stop playing it for laughs, constantly pulling faces and rolling his eyes. Arlene Phillips picked up on it straight away: 'Jason was waltzing with his face more than he was with his feet,' she said. Wood was clearly stung, and realized he had to rely on choreography rather than comedy. By week two's Rumba, he was in much better shape. 'Last week it was like dragging round a jumbo jet,' he said, 'this week I was a little cruiser', and Len Goodman agreed: 'From a caterpillar to a butterfly!' Even Phillips was converted, calling Wood's performance 'sensual' (which prompted some wag in the audience to yell out, 'Put your glasses on!').

But they still didn't score highly, and the audience vote wasn't enough to save them. 'Nobody wants to go out first,' said Wood, 'but I have to say I've enjoyed every minute. Dancing with Kylie was like having a little bit of magic in my arms.'

NAME Jason Wood
DAY JOB Stand-up comedian and musical impressionist
DANCE PARTNER Kylie Jones
BEST DANCE Their first-week Waltz to 'Three Times a Lady', which gained 21 points.
WORST DANCE Their Rumba in week two impressed some judges, but prompted Craig Revel Horwood to award a stingy two points.
THE JUDGES SAID Craig: 'Jason was cheesy, lumpy and awkward. He should take this competition a little more seriously.'
HOW DID THEY DO? First to leave series one, in the third week.

Camilla Dallerup

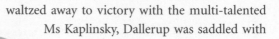

Danish dancing queen Camilla Dallerup found herself not just competing in a dance competition when she entered Strictly Come Dancing *but also starring in an unexpected soap opera.*

When her nine-year relationship with her personal and professional partner Brendan Cole came to an end during the show, the press was quick to point the finger at Natasha Kaplinsky as 'the other woman', and interest in all parties became intense. Sadly for Dallerup, most of her involvement with the show was destined to be off the dance floor, because she was unlucky in her choice of celebrity partner. While Cole waltzed away to victory with the multi-talented Ms Kaplinsky, Dallerup was saddled with David Dickinson, a man to whom the words 'rhythm' and 'co-ordination' were like a foreign language. Unsurprisingly, they were the first couple to be knocked out of the show, sparing us all the spectacle of a tug-of-love between Cole and Dallerup.

Dallerup has been dancing since the age of two, when her mother took her to her first dance classes at home in Aalborg, Denmark. She took to it like a duck to water, and by the age of six was sneaking into dance competitions that, technically, you had to be eight to enter. She won the Danish Junior Championships at the age of 12, and started visiting the UK to compete. She met Brendan Cole, their partnership blossomed and, over the course of the next few years, they scooped most of the significant Latin titles in the world.

After the trials and traumas of the first series of *Strictly Come Dancing*, Dallerup picked herself up, dusted herself off and, most significantly, found herself a new professional dance partner in the shape of Ian Waite – who partnered Denise Lewis to near-victory. And this time she was more fortunate in her dance partner, training with Roger Black who, unlike David Dickinson, was not only physically fit but also possessed of an innate sense of rhythm. In series three, she did well again, partnering James Martin all the way to the semi-final. This year Camilla is dancing with Ray Fearon.

Anton du Beke

He's the gracious king of the ballroom floor and, thanks to Strictly Come Dancing, *he's also become the housewives' favourite.*

'I wish every woman on the planet could have half an hour with Anton du Beke,' gushed Lesley Garrett at the end of her stint on the first series of *Strictly Come Dancing*. While that may not be entirely practical, du Beke certainly made an impression on both his celebrity partners, not to mention the viewing public. Garrett liked him so much that she invited him to dance with her at gala concerts long after the show was finished. Esther Rantzen, du Beke's partner in series two, was similarly smitten. So keen was she on maximising their training time that she whisked him away on a three-day Caribbean cruise.

Du Beke is one of the stars of contemporary ballroom; with his professional partner, Erin Boag, he was named ICDT Classic Champion in 2003, and has a fistful of other awards and titles under his belt. He started dancing relatively late, at the age of 14, and at 17 decided to specialize in ballroom. He rose quickly through the ranks, and as well as being a champion, he became a sought-after teacher throughout the UK.

Du Beke emerged as one of the outstanding characters of the first series, largely due to his strictly-for-laughs friendship with Lesley Garrett. They fell on top of each other in rehearsals, they shouted at each other, they whipped up rivalry with the other contestants and appeared to be having the time of their lives. Du Beke admitted that, 'This is the best thing I've ever done, and the highlight is being with Lesley every day.' That chemistry took them to the semi-finals, but despite superior dancing skills, they never made it to the final.

The second-series partnership with Esther Rantzen was never as fiery, but they clearly got on well. 'She's so wonderful,' said gallant du Beke. 'The Esther you've seen on telly over the last few years is nothing like the Esther you see in the studio. She's incredible fun.' And in series three, du Beke was perfectly matched with Patsy Palmer, whom he coached into real ballroom elegance. They made it to the quarter final, and he pronounced her 'the most completely wonderful person to be with.' What a gent. Let's see if his series four partner, Jan Raven, feels the same.

Paul Killick

There's a bad boy in every gang, and Paul 'Killer' Killick established early in the first series that he was determined to fulfil that role in Strictly Come Dancing.

Bursting onto the floor in a leopardskin jacket, he executed a nifty Cha Cha Cha with Verona Joseph before lifting her up, spinning her around and depositing her on the floor. The judges gasped with disapproval (the dancers are supposed to keep a toe on the floor at all times), but still scored the

performance highly, convinced that 'rules were made to be broken'. Killick was always going to be the loose cannon in *Strictly Come Dancing*, his reputation in the dance world rests upon his excellence in the Rumba and the Paso Doble – the most dramatic Latin dances.

Londoner Killick was moving to music before he could walk but a trip to the cinema took an unexpected turn when Killick's grandfather heard music and discovered the world-famous Peggy Spencer's Dancing School. Spencer, a veteran of the original *Come Dancing*, took Paul under her wing and nurtured what soon emerged as an extraordinary talent.

Killick trained throughout his teens until he turned professional in 1994. He then danced with Hanna Karttunen until their retirement; together they have a cupboard bursting with trophies. He didn't find it easy to adapt to the amateur competitiveness of the show, berating Verona Joseph for her apparent lack of commitment. It didn't matter that she was working full time in *Holby City*; Killick expected nothing short of 100 per cent. But what they lacked in technical perfection, they more than made up for in temperament. Killick's appearances were the most dramatic, explosive dances across the two series. When he and Hanna Karttunen did a farewell Samba, her in feathers, him dressed in bright red, we could see what we'd missed by voting him off the show.

Unfortunately he didn't fare much better in the second series, when he was paired with Carol Vorderman, and crashed out of the competition after the second week. But Killick did quit the show on a high and soon opened his own London dance studio.

Erin Boag

She's the epitome of grace and effortless style in her professional dancing life. But how would Erin Boag, the queen of ballroom, cope with a rugby player, a comedian and an athlete leading her around the floor?

Erin Boag is a very determined woman. At the age of three, she persuaded her mother to take her to dance classes, and quickly mastered ballet, tap, jazz, ballroom and Latin. In her teens, she moved from her native New Zealand to Australia. When she moved to London she announced to her then-partner that she would be dancing in the International Dance Championships within a year and, although he laughed, 12 months later she was there. It sounds easy, but it was anything but. Boag split with her partner, and found herself alone in a foreign city. 'That was tough. I took four jobs to support myself; money was scarce. I remember sitting on a bus with my last pound, not knowing whether to laugh or cry.' Then destiny, in the shape of Anton du Beke, came along, and they formed a partnership that took them to the top of the ballroom world. They turned professional in 2002; in 2003 they became the IDTA Classic Champions.

But, as *Strictly Come Dancing* proves again and again, professional success in any sphere is no guarantee of victory in the studio. In series one, Boag was paired with Martin Offiah: could she turn a hulking rugby player into a graceful ballroom butterfly? Amazingly, the answer seemed to be 'yes', transforming him from a stiff, frightened-looking dummy into a graceful dancer. In series two, Boag had a different challenge with Julian Clary. Again, Clary wasn't too comfortable in the ballroom, but Boag put him at ease, and their sense of fun soon shone through. By the middle of the series, Clary had improved, and even his arch-enemy, Craig Revel Horwood was forced to admit it. 'Erin's such a good teacher,' raved Clary. 'She's so persistently positive, and I absorb her confidence.' Some critics complained that Clary's result relied largely on his personality – a charge that couldn't be levelled at Boag's series three partner, Colin Jackson, with whom she waltzed effortlessly to second place. She's staying in the sporting arena this year, partnering goalkeeping legend Peter Schmeichel.

Brendan Cole

Of all the professional dancers in Strictly Come Dancing, *only one threatened to overshadow the 'real' celebrities in terms of press interest, and that was Brendan Cole.*

Apart from being a great dancer and very good-looking, in series one he pulled out the trump card – at least, in PR terms – of splitting up with his fiancée and dance partner, Camilla Dallerup, and sparking rumours of a relationship with his co-competitor, Natasha Kaplinsky. There was no doubt that they were the best dancers on the floor – but their runaway success with the public owed as much to the Cole-Kaplinsky chemistry, and the acres of press coverage it attracted.

Brendan Cole is the opposite of the clichéd image of the male ballroom dancer as a wooden, sexless dummy. A strapping six-foot-one New Zealander who started off working on building sites, he arrived at the BBC oozing sex appeal, singing the praises of the Rumba 'because it's two bodies trying to create a moment', and a track record to prove it. His professional relationship with Camilla Dallerup had quickly become personal. 'We'd only just started dancing together, and I flew to Denmark to train for the Blackpool championships. We both agreed that the relationship was to be purely professional. I stayed in Camilla's flat in a bed on the opposite side of the room. That lasted five minutes.'

Dancing together, Cole and Dallerup represented Denmark and New Zealand, but on *Strictly Come Dancing*, they were competing against each other. Their nine-year relationship foundered, and the press have speculated ever since about whether or not they will get back together. Whatever the truth of Cole's offscreen romancing, there was no doubt that he and Natasha Kaplinsky were magic on the dance floor. The first few weeks were tense: Kaplinsky was deeply unsure about the project, and Cole was, she said, 'gentle and polite at first, but after a few weeks he turned into a complete brute'. The caveman act worked. 'She was ridiculous,' he says, 'and I responded by treading on eggshells. But soon it was time to turn up the heat and get on with it.'

Cole and Kaplinsky danced their way to victory, and when he returned in series two, there was a high expectation that he would do the same with Sarah Manners. But they never gelled and there were rows, tears and recriminations. It didn't really matter: they were knocked out after five weeks, and Cole admitted that they had never got on as dancers. And the magic failed to return again with Fiona Phillips, the second morning TV presenter to swoon in his arms; they were knocked out in the fourth week. This year King Cole will be trying to reclaim his crown with celebrity partner Claire King.

Hanna Karttunen

There are surprises in Strictly Come Dancing, *there are sometimes miracles, and then there is Christopher Parker. The fact that Hanna Karttunen managed to steer him to the final still ranks as the biggest surprise of the show, given that the young EastEnders star could barely dance a step when he began training.*

By the end of the show he could, perhaps, dance two steps – a tribute to Karttunen's perseverance – but the combination of their two personalities proved irresistible to viewers. We all know that young Mr Parker can mobilise huge armies of fans with one blink of his puppy-dog eyes, but Karttunen's own fiery charms and eternal optimism contributed hugely to the partnership. Not for nothing is she known, with scant regard for zoology, as 'the Finnish tigress' in the dance world. The nickname seemed particularly appropriate as the judges rained down condemnation on Parker, and an affronted Karttunen took him under her protective wing.

As Paul Killick's professional partner, Karttunen has won most of the significant titles in the Latin dance world – and they bowed out in spectacular style by retiring from competition during the series, and showing the world what they were made of with an unforgettable exhibition Samba.

For the rest of the series, she focused her energies on Christopher Parker, pulling him through each successive dance as if her life depended it, covering all his mistakes with fancy footwork, comforting him when the judges were mean. Somehow, it was

enough. Week after week, even when they ended up at the bottom of the leader board, the public kept voting them back in to compete again.

Perhaps the effort was too much for her, as Karttunen did not return to dance in *Strictly Come Dancing*.

John Byrnes

John Byrnes joined Strictly Come Dancing *as a consultant, adviser and go-between for the BBC in its negotiations with the professional dance world. 'There was a great concern among dancers, and dance organisations, that we should not be shown in a bad light. We live on our reputations; if they are damaged it can ruin our livelihood.*

So I needed a lot of assurance from the BBC that this wasn't going to be a mickey-take. We'd just emerged from that horrendous period when everyone thought ballroom dancing was tacky, all sequinned jumpsuits and huge collars, and we didn't want to do anything that was going to set us back.'

Byrnes advised Creative Head of Format Entertainment Karen Smith on a range of technical points, from costuming to rehearsal time. He also introduced her to some dancers. 'I found myself in the unenviable position of representing the dance world to the BBC, and the BBC to the dance world. There were a lot of phone calls and emails going back and forth, and we were all very nervous. When we heard that they were going to call it *Strictly Come Dancing*, it started all over again; much as I love the film *Strictly Ballroom* (and I have a lot of friends who were in it), I didn't want to get involved in something that was aiming to get a cheap laugh out of ballroom dancing. We've all been dancing since we were kids, and we take it seriously.'

Eventually, the format was licked into shape to everyone's satisfaction – and Byrnes found himself partnering Claire Sweeney. 'Claire wanted to

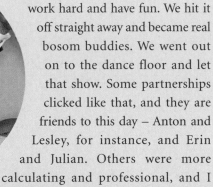

work hard and have fun. We hit it off straight away and became real bosom buddies. We went out on to the dance floor and let that show. Some partnerships clicked like that, and they are friends to this day – Anton and Lesley, for instance, and Erin and Julian. Others were more calculating and professional, and I think it showed on screen.'

As the show launched the dance world still wondered whether it would be a curse or a blessing. 'There were people telling me I'd made a big mistake, that I was going to drag dance down. After a few weeks, they changed their tune. They saw that the show was working, and that their businesses were flourishing as a result, and now everyone agrees that it was the best thing to happen to dance for years.'

Byrnes opted out of the second series; his wife, dancer Jane Lyttleton-Byrnes, had recently given birth to a son, and his dance school demanded more

time than the show would allow. 'I was sorry not to be in the second series, but I'm still very satisfied at my part in the show. I've never been involved in anything on that level before, and even though I look back now and wonder how I managed, it was a tremendous experience.'

Kylie Jones

Blink and you'd have missed Kylie Jones – she was partnered with Jason Wood in the first series and was the first of the dancers to be knocked out of the show. That's a shame, because, on that slender showing, she was one of the more instantly likeable characters among the professional team.

She started dancing at the age of seven in her native Manchester, and by ten she was competing across the country. In 1989 she and her partner Stephen Sysum won the International Juvenile Ballroom Championship, and went on to even greater heights, winning the Open British Juvenile Ballroom championships three times in a row.

At 16, Jones changed partners and, with Jonathan Crossley, became twice World Amateur Ballroom Champions. They turned professional, taught and performed all over the world until dissolving the partnership in 2002. *Strictly Come Dancing* wasn't Jones's first TV appearance: at the tender age of 11 she was teaching John Leslie how to dance on *Blue Peter*, and later made an appearance on sports quiz *They Think It's All Over*.

Her experience on *Strictly Come Dancing* was short, but sweet. Jones and Wood clearly got on like a house on fire despite his obvious nerves and lack of dancing ability. When they were knocked out, Jones was gracious in defeat. 'He danced the best he could,' she said. 'He really couldn't have done any more.'

Series Two

Roger Black

Roger Black certainly looked the part – fit, athletic, and not averse to see-through shirts. But would the judges favour his footwork?

NAME Roger Black
DAY JOB Olympic 400-metre sprinter, BBC sports presenter
DANCE PARTNER Camilla Dallerup
BEST DANCE The Foxtrot in week four, which scored 29 out of 40. Bruno compared Black to 'a matinee idol', while Craig said it was so perfect he was 'bored'.
WORST DANCE The Rumba in week six. Arlene said Black was dancing like 'a plank of wood'.
THE JUDGES SAID Arlene: 'You're gorgeous to watch, you have a lot of style, but I think you've got a long way to go.' Craig: 'Clumpy, ungainly, no bounce.'
HOW DID THEY DO? Knocked out after the sixth show.

There were two professional athletes in the second series of *Strictly Come Dancing*, and it might have seemed that they had an unfair advantage. Roger Black and Denise Lewis were never going to have any problems in the fitness department, unlike some who were puffing and panting when they came off the dance floor. But physical fitness does not ensure grace, rhythm or co-ordination. Training, however, proved a problem for Black, who was unable to commit to as much as his partner, Camilla Dallerup, would have liked. The lack of practice time became so frustrating that she had to accompany him on a trip to Cannes. It paid off. Black's dancing in the first few weeks of the show impressed the judges, and the scores were respectably high.

But just when everyone expected Black and Dallerup to soar into the upper echelons of the competition, something went wrong. Perhaps it was lack of practice, perhaps Black had just reached the limit of his dance talent, but in the sixth show both the Waltz and the Rumba were slammed by the judges. Even a clever bit of costume stagecraft, in which Black unhooked a huge floating panel of red chiffon over Dallerup's black dress, failed to tip the balance, and they were knocked out.

Black admitted that, as Dallerup had pointed out, he had a tendency to morph into *The Office*'s David Brent when under pressure, but he relished the competition. 'In the end, and this sounds corny, I have made a friend. Camilla and my wife, Jules, have become good friends, and that will last. There was nothing bad about doing *Strictly Come Dancing*.'

Sarah Manners

Stepping out from behind the casualty desk, Sarah Manners placed herself in the hands – and on the thighs – of Brendan Cole. Would she share in his second victory?

The *Strictly Come Dancing* experience isn't always easy for the girls from *Holby City* hospital. Verona Joseph was hampered by filming schedules in the first series, but Sarah Manners, who plays *Casualty*'s receptionist Bex, was in the middle of one of her heaviest-ever storylines in the show, in which her character was raped. Added to that, she quickly developed a tempestuous relationship with her dance partner Brendan Cole, which led to a spectacular falling-out. 'I saw him on the BBC2 show saying that dancing with me was like dancing with a brick wall,' said Manners, 'and I just burst into tears. Afterwards he was very apologetic, and wished he hadn't said it.' The pair managed to make up in time for their Paso Doble in the fourth week, a gothic extravaganza to Evanescence's 'Bring Me to Life', in which Manners revealed she would 'sacrifice myself on Brendan Cole's thighs'.

Training continued to be a problem, however, as Manners was stuck in Bristol filming *Casualty* when she should have been travelling up to London or Blackpool to train. In the first series, it was Brendan Cole's obvious chemistry with his dance partner Natasha Kaplinsky that led him to victory; but it seemed that was not going to be repeated in series two. After a troubled five weeks, and a disappointing Samba in which her heel got caught in her dress, Manners and Cole were knocked out. 'I'm not relieved,' said Manners, 'because that sounds like I was hating it. But I do feel like there's a weight lifted off my shoulders in that it was very stressful. I was very busy at work. I loved doing the show.'

NAME Sarah Manners
DAY JOB Actor, plays Bex Reynolds in *Casualty*
DANCE PARTNER Brendan Cole
BEST DANCE After a stormy week of public rows and minimal training, the bickering pair made up for long enough to execute an impressive Tango to 'Hernando's Hideaway', scoring 31.
WORST DANCE The Rumba in week two was 'stiff and icy' according to Bruno, and only scored 23, which was the same for their Samba in week five.
THE JUDGES SAID Len: 'You didn't have your heart in it.' Bruno: 'You have to let yourself go.' Arlene: 'Where was the sex?'
HOW DID THEY DO? Knocked out after the fifth show.

Julian Clary

Julian Clary wasn't the most obvious choice for Strictly Come Dancing. *He was the first to admit he couldn't dance and, to make matters worse, he made the claim that he had never touched a woman in his life.*

NAME Julian Clary
DAY JOB Comedian
DANCE PARTNER Erin Boag
BEST DANCE 28 out of 40 for the sixth-week Waltz.
WORST DANCE A disastrous start with the first-week Cha Cha Cha, which scored only 19.
THE JUDGES SAID Bruno: 'Light as Tinkerbell!'
Len: 'As soon as you got your maracas out, I knew we were in for a treat.'
HOW DID THEY DO? Miraculously made it to the second-series final.

More seriously, his reputation as a loose cannon on live television had made entertainment producers nervous since some unfortunate remarks about Norman Lamont's red box at the British Comedy Awards in 1993. He was, without doubt, the wild card for the second series – and he ended up as one of its biggest stars.

From the start, it was obvious that he was not a natural. 'I used to disco-dance years ago,' he said. 'I came off the dance floor at a rough disco in Magaluf, and some vicious queen said, "Well, you realize you can't dance...". So I thought, all right, I won't dance any more. It was difficult to persuade myself to do this because I've always believed that I just can't dance.'

Less determined women than Erin might have given up at this point, but the public realized that Clary was prepared to give it his best shot, and Boag responded by pushing him to his limits. 'It's 100 per cent Erin. She's such a good teacher, so relentlessly positive.' Clary's scores shot up for the second-week quickstep, and from then on they were in the running.

And his performance didn't end after the dance. His confrontations with the judges – particularly with Craig Revell Horwood – became a weekly treat. In the fourth week, after Revell Horwood's stinging assessment of his Paso Doble, Clary rounded on him with, 'You wouldn't know a Paso Doble if you sat on one!'. From then on, it was war.

In the final, Clary Samba'd out saying, 'The show has brought real joy to my life.' And it has: within weeks he was back on live prime-time TV, presenting BBC1's lottery show.

Jill Halfpenny

Strictly Come Dancing *already had strong links with* EastEnders *before Jill Halfpenny joined the second series. 'I'd seen how hard Christopher worked, so I had no illusions it would be an easy ride.'*

'When they cast the second series, my name went into the hat along with five or six others; they knew that they wanted someone from *EastEnders* to be in it, because of the BBC1 connection.' Halfpenny was chosen, and from the very beginning it was clear that she had the potential to go all the way to the final.

'I did a bit of ballet and tap when I was a little girl, so I wasn't scared of dancing, and I had a good sense of rhythm. But I had never done ballroom before, so when I started rehearsing with Darren [Bennett] I was really worried. It's funny how skills you learned in your childhood come flooding back. Darren's a very strict, precise teacher, but I'm a hard worker too, and like to get things right, so we clicked from the start.'

Halfpenny left *EastEnders* the week before going into training for *Strictly Come Dancing*, a happy schedule coincidence that eased her workload considerably. 'The training was hard, but at least I could just concentrate on that, unlike other people who were juggling other jobs. But nothing could prepare me for the first show. Standing backstage waiting to go on was the most nerve-wracking experience of my life. I had complete and utter stage fright; I seriously wanted to run away when our names were announced. I felt completely out of my depth. That's never happened to me before.'

As weeks went by, Halfpenny became more determined to get to the final. 'It wasn't so much that I wanted to win; I just didn't want to miss a show. The final was really hard; Darren was ill and we were both so tired – but adrenalin kicked in just when we needed it.'

NAME Jill Halfpenny
DAY JOB Actor in *Byker Grove* and *EastEnders*, more recently in the West End in *Chicago*
DANCE PARTNER Darren Bennett
BEST DANCE The judges gave their first (and so far their only) 40 out of 40 to Jill and Darren's Jive to 'I'm Still Standing' in the series-two final.
WORST DANCE 27 for their first-week Waltz.
THE JUDGES SAID Arlene: 'As a choreographer, I bow to you, Jill. The warmth was phenomenal.'
Len: 'I'm overwhelmed. Best dance of the series.'
HOW DID THEY DO? Winners of the second series and of the Champion of Champions Christmas special programme.

Diarmuid Gavin

Diarmuid Gavin may have green fingers – but it soon became apparent that he also has two left feet. Could the bad boy of gardening cultivate new talents on the dance floor?

NAME Diarmuid Gavin
DAY JOB Garden designer and TV presenter
DANCE PARTNER Nicole Cutler
BEST DANCE Despite a hamstring injury sustained on another dance floor, Gavin managed a personal best of 17 out of 40 for his Paso Doble in the fourth show.
WORST DANCE Where to begin? The first three dances polled only 12 out of 40 between them.
THE JUDGES SAID Craig: 'Crude and lumpy.'
Bruno: 'You're holding a beautiful girl, not a potted plant. A Quickstep is supposed to be like a soufflé, light and fluffy. This was a spotted dick.'
HOW DID THEY DO? Knocked out after the fourth show.

Diarmuid Gavin never had very high hopes of his chances on *Strictly Come Dancing*. Even during the training, he complained, 'It's not working. I'm fat, hairy and pale. I'm from Dublin and I'm not black so I haven't got any sense of rhythm. At the end of the day, I can't bear to look at myself in the mirror.' Being white and Irish isn't much of a reason for being unable to dance – ask Michael Flatley – but having absolutely no sense of rhythm whatsoever certainly doesn't help. Gavin's dance partner, Nicole Cutler, was visibly frustrated in rehearsals by his inability to hear the beat, or to make his body move in anything like time. But, as it turned out, Quentin Willson was even worse – and so Gavin managed to stay in the show until the fourth week.

When the axe finally fell, Gavin was 'disappointed and embarrassed' – but he could have taken comfort in the fact that his considerable fan base had kept him in for so long. Ultimately he accepted that the judges may have had a point. 'They're probably right,' he said. 'I felt it should have been about people who couldn't dance, learning progressively, week by week. But I didn't hear any of that in what they were saying.'

It was Gavin's self-consciousness that did for him. Nicole Cutler said he was much better without the camera on him. 'I can't understand this man,' she said. 'He's extremely sexy, he's loved in Britain and Ireland, and housewives adore him, but he's the most self-conscious person.' Something good came out of the experience, though. Gavin's eight-month-pregnant wife, Justine, spent the entire series 'rolling around on the carpet laughing at me.'

Esther Rantzen

Before Strictly Come Dancing, *Esther Rantzen described herself as 'a little old lady with a hump' and her clumsy gait and long feet, as like 'an elephant on skis'. Five weeks pressed against Anton du Beke changed all that.*

He ruthlessly straightened her shoulders, lengthened her neck, and taught her to glide round the floor. The result? Esther waltzed elegantly to 'Moon River', swooping and dipping in a dress to suit Ginger Rogers. Arch-bitch Arlene Phillips approved her first performance as classy and professional.

Things started well for Rantzen and du Beke with an elegant Waltz in the first week but their second-week Rumba was a mess. 'The Rumba is "the dance of love", and much as I loved Anton I was terrified by his commands to push out my bust and stick out my bum. I had to do something to distract him, so I bought myself a cheap red wig.' She christened it 'Sharon' in honour of Mrs Osbourne. It did the trick and the audience voted to keep her in. The third week she had to dance the Tango, with its sharp, staccato movements. Terrified that Sharon might be shaken loose, she abandoned the lucky wig and put a garter on her thigh instead. Rantzen strutted her stuff in a Tango that Craig Revel Horwood described as 'technically an absolute disaster, but dramatically triumphant'. Sadly, it was too late, and low scores from the judges and weak public support booted her out. Rantzen, however, was still a winner. 'It changed my life,' she says. 'After the show I took Sharon to my hairdressers, they copied the colour and I've been a redhead ever since. Whenever I'm at a supermarket check-out people say, "Aren't you lucky, you're a natural dancer." I never tell them my dancing is as natural as my hair!'. All the exercise lost four inches off her waist, 'My children say I look ten years younger. Why bother with a gym when you can go dancing with Anton du Beke?'

NAME Esther Rantzen OBE
DAY JOB TV presenter, creator and chair of Childline
DANCE PARTNER Anton du Beke
BEST DANCE The Waltz in week one impressed the judges, who gave them 24 points.
WORST DANCE Fancy footwork got the better of Esther in the second and third shows; the Rumba and the Tango both polled a poor 16.
THE JUDGES SAID Arlene outbitched herself for Rantzen's Rumba. 'It's meant to be the dance of love,' she said, 'but it seemed as though it was the dance of desperation.'
HOW DID THEY DO? Knocked out after the third show.

Aled Jones

He was used to walking in the air, but had stayed away from the dance floor. Then Aled Jones amazed everyone by making it all the way to the semi-final.

NAME Aled Jones
DAY JOB Singer and television presenter
DANCE PARTNER Lilia Kopylova
BEST DANCE Overcoming injury and memory-loss in the Jive in week three, 32 out of 40.
WORST DANCE A disappointing Foxtrot in week four scored only 25.
THE JUDGES SAID Len: 'All balls and no heels.' Craig: 'Laboured and lumbering.'
HOW DID THEY DO? A surprise departure from the semi-final.

'I really couldn't dance before I did the show,' says Aled Jones. 'I was so bad that I didn't even dance on my wedding night, I just propped up the bar.' But after missing out on a shot at the first series – he was touring Australia at the time – Jones was 'chomping at the bit' when the producers asked him to come back for the second. 'Everyone laughed at the thought of me dancing but I knew that at the very least it would teach me to move a bit, and get me fit.' During the course of training, Jones lost two and a half stone, more than anyone else who has featured in the show.

'I started off as a complete novice. To make matters worse, I was on a 36-date UK tour throughout the series, so we had to fit training in around my schedule. Lilia [Kopylova] had to follow me all over the country, which was hard for her. In our first lesson I had to learn a Cha Cha Cha, to Ricky Martin's 'She Bangs', and I came out thinking, well, there goes my *Songs of Praise* contract. This is far too sexy. In fact, the *Songs of Praise* audience turned out to be my best supporters. I think they appreciated seeing the real me.'

To everyone's surprise, not least his own, Jones turned out to be a decent dancer and a favourite with judges and viewers alike. He fought through round after round, despite some hairy moments. 'During our Jive, I completely forgot the steps, and had to stand there punching the air.'

Despite being knocked out in the semi-final, Jones returned for the Christmas special, wearing a white bejewelled catsuit. 'I'm a lot more confident on stage now. And now people come up to me and talk about something other than the bloody Snowman. It's about time.'

Denise Lewis

The Olympic heptathlete needed something to cheer her up after injury forced her to pull out of Athens 2004. But was Strictly Come Dancing *just what the doctor ordered?*

'Athens was soul-destroying,' says Denise Lewis. 'I needed something that would take my mind off things and make me laugh. *Strictly Come Dancing* came at such a good time. I could throw my energy into something completely different.'

And that's exactly what she did. Training with dance partner Ian Waite turned her from a lean, mean athletic machine into a vision of grace and agility on the dance floor. 'This may sound corny, but I've always wanted to be a dancer. Ever since I was a little girl I've loved jiggling around.' That 'jiggling' took a 12-year-old Lewis onto local stages in the Midlands, where she tap-danced to 'Singin' in the Rain'. But eventually she had to choose between dance and athletics, and the rest is history. 'I had to make my mind up, and knew deep down that dancing wasn't my strongest point.'

Waite drew out her latent talent though, and within weeks Lewis was gliding around with the best of them. Throughout successive rounds Lewis's technique and confidence improved. She went into extra training – once an Olympian, always an Olympian – and took ballet lessons to improve her poise. The training paid off, and in the semi-final Lewis tangoed her way into the judges' good books.

After being pipped to the post by Jill Halfpenny in the final, Lewis revealed that she nearly hadn't made it onto the dance floor. 'I suffer from an excruciating stomach disorder called Irritable Bowel Syndrome. It's caused by stress, so the first time I was due to perform in front of millions of viewers I was sure an attack would happen. We stepped out, the music began and – nothing. I hope it means I've finally overcome it.'

NAME Denise Lewis MBE
DAY JOB Olympic heptathlete
DANCE PARTNER Ian Waite
BEST DANCE An exceptional 38 out of 40 for the final Quickstep.
WORST DANCE Their Jive to Rachel Stevens's 'Some Girls' only scored 25 in the third week.
THE JUDGES SAID Bruno: 'The poise of a panther playing with her prey.' Craig: 'Very, very exciting. I can't take my eyes off you.'
HOW DID THEY DO? A few points short of overall victory in the final.

Carol Vorderman

Some people sit back and let the judges' comments wash over them. Not Carol Vorderman, who, after a shock exit in the second week, hit back with some comments of her own.

NAME Carol Vorderman MBE

DAY JOB *Countdown* presenter, all-round TV personality and maths whizz

DANCE PARTNER Paul Killick

BEST DANCE 22 out of 40 for their first-week Waltz. They lost marks on technique.

WORST DANCE 20 out of 40 for their second-week Rumba – during which Vorderman sustained a cartilage injury. Skin-tight, flesh-coloured outfits didn't even win over the judges.

THE JUDGES SAID Arlene: 'I didn't see any connection between you. You lacked emotion.'

HOW DID THEY DO? Knocked out after the second show.

Before the start of series two, there were plenty of people who thought Carol Vorderman could walk off with the *Strictly Come Dancing* trophy. She was, after all, well known for her love of parties and sparkly dresses; surely dancing would be second nature? She could also rely on her massive *Countdown* audience to get the votes in. But, in the event, she and partner Paul Killick were booted off after the second show. What went wrong?

Writing in the press after she left the show, Vorderman let rip with an invective that left no doubt as to where she thought the trouble lay. She accused Arlene Phillips of 'undisguised animosity' and described her as 'Sharon Osbourne, without the charm'. This led to a war of words between the two women, but it was too late to save Vorderman, whose chance of dance glory had gone.

It's a shame because from the two performances she gave, she had what it takes to go a lot further. But perhaps it was just as well she took an early bath, because an injury in the second week meant that training could have been a problem. She tore some cartilage beside her ribcage during the Rumba, and, despite smiling through the rest of the show, she went straight to casualty the next day. 'Paul's nickname is "the Killer", she said, 'and now I know why!'

It was a painful end to a beautiful friendship. 'When I first met Paul,' she said, 'he introduced himself, "Hi, I'm Paul. Put your leg around my waist, hold the back of my neck, and lean back as far as you can when I tell you to." Twenty minutes later I hobbled away like Nora Batty's bendy sister.'

Quentin Willson

Some people are natural dancers. Some people can learn to dance through effort and training. And then there's Quentin Willson...

'My wife said it would be fantastic,' said Quentin Willson when he went into training for *Strictly Come Dancing*. 'I think she was hoping that it would make me less clumsy and stop me stepping on the dog. I really am the worst dancer.' This was not false modesty. Despite the best efforts of Willson's long-suffering training partner, Hazel Newberry, nothing on earth was ever going to turn the ugly duckling of the dance floor into an elegant swan.

Willson tried hard in training, but from the moment he stepped out for his first-week Cha Cha Cha it was obvious that he was not long for the show. The judges served up some of their most withering put-downs (see below), and, unfortunately, the viewers agreed. 'I think I now know that I am to dancing what Frank Bruno is to English literature,' said Willson when the verdict was delivered. 'Builders on the street have been congratulating me on my bravery. The most disappointing thing is that I let Hazel down.'

But Willson was a good loser, and he chalked the whole thing up to experience. 'When I was first asked to do this, my initial reaction was yes, of course, I can do it. It's just a question of putting one foot in front of the other. But I found it the most difficult thing I've ever done. I've loved every single minute of it, and I'm going to miss it. But success in life is knowing what your limitations are.' So Willson went back to stepping on the dog – but seven pounds lighter, and minus two inches on his waist.

NAME Quentin Willson
DAY JOB *Top Gear* presenter
DANCE PARTNER Hazel Newberry
BEST/WORST DANCE There was only one, the Cha Cha Cha – not the easiest dance for a novice to begin with. The judges only managed a grand total of eight marks – the lowest score to date on *Strictly Come Dancing*.
THE JUDGES SAID Craig: 'Britain's worst dancer!' Bruno: 'It was like watching a Robin Reliant with a Ferrari.'
HOW DID THEY DO? Knocked out after the first show.

Darren Bennett

As one half of the winning team of the second series, Darren Bennett added one more trophy to an already enormous collection. With his dance partner (and wife) Lilia Kopylova he's won the International and British Youth Championships and, immediately after turning professional in 2003, they won the British Rising Star Professional Championships at their first attempt. Within a year they were ranking sixth in the world series.

Sheffield-born Bennett has been dancing since the age of six – which didn't come as much surprise to his parents, both of whom were professional dancers. He'd done so well as a junior that he had his first taste of TV fame in the mid-90s, appearing on the original *Come Dancing* show. His twin brother, Dale (yet another dancer in the

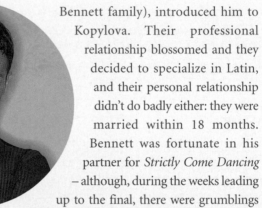

Bennett family), introduced him to Kopylova. Their professional relationship blossomed and they decided to specialize in Latin, and their personal relationship didn't do badly either: they were married within 18 months. Bennett was fortunate in his partner for *Strictly Come Dancing* – although, during the weeks leading up to the final, there were grumblings from some quarters that Jill Halfpenny was actually too good to be in the competition, having had some previous dance experience. Halfpenny was dismissive ('It's just a bit of gossip'), but Bennett was more philosophical. 'It's all about putting in a good performance every week so that they don't have a chance to give us a bad mark,' he said. And he wasn't wrong: they were the first couple ever to score a perfect 40 for their Jive to 'I'm Still Standing' in the final.

Things didn't work out quite so well in the third series, when he was partnered with Gloria Hunniford. They worked hard together, and Hunniford was starting to blossom on the dance floor, but in the end the competition was just too stiff, and they were out in the third week. Bennett will be hoping to go further this year, as he partners former Spice Girl Emma Bunton.

Nicole Cutler

Nicole Cutler didn't get much of a chance to show off her skills in the second series of Strictly Come Dancing. *Partnered with Diarmuid Gavin, she was soon out of the running – but not before she'd had a brave stab at turning the gardener into a dancer.*

'Diarmuid was never going to be a natural dancer,' she says, 'but he made up for it in other ways. He tried so hard, and he was very willing to learn – which is really all you can ask for as a teacher. I do a lot of professional teaching, and this experience really stretched me. Usually you're starting off with someone who has basic dance ability – a sense of rhythm, at least – otherwise they wouldn't be there. But Diarmuid just couldn't hear the rhythm at all. I had to think of new ways of explaining the dance to him, in terms that he would understand. In the end, I related all the choreography to gardening – I got him to think of the dance floor in terms of borders and lawns, with the steps as different plants, and so on. It was starting to work. In our final week, when we did the Paso Doble, he was starting to make real progress. It was frustrating that we were voted off that week, because I think we were heading for a breakthrough.'

Nicole Cutler has been dancing all her life: she started off in her native South Africa then scaled the heights of the professional Latin American circuit after she moved to the UK at the age of 18. For ten years she danced with her husband, Matthew (one of the professional dancers in the third series of *Strictly Come Dancing*), and together they became All England Professional Champions in 2004. Now she's partnered by Robin Sewell. 'Doing *Strictly Come Dancing* was a very useful experience for me,' she says. 'On a personal level, it's boosted my business: so many people want to learn how to dance, and to see professional dancers. But it's done a lot for the whole image of the business, too. People used to think we just ponced around in sequins, covered in fake tan. Now they can see how hard we work. Mind you, *Strictly Come Dancing* is ridiculously hard work. We're teaching a new dance in one week, from the start to performance; that's nearly impossible. We'd never have to do that in the real world.' Cutler is back in the fourth series partnering news presenter Nicholas Owen.

Lilia Kopylova

Diminutive Russian Lilia Kopylova (alias Mrs Darren Bennett) began dancing in her native Moscow at the age of nine, when her grandmother signed her up for ballroom lessons at school. Instantly hooked, she never looked back – and by the age of 15 she was already a ballroom and Latin champion.

As if this wasn't enough, she'd also won titles for figure skating and gymnastics; they take their competitions seriously in Russia. A chance meeting with Bennett's dancer brother Dale in Denmark brought her to England, where she had a 15-minute tryout with Darren – and they've been dancing (and living) together ever since.

So what's it like being a private couple, as well as a public one? 'We have two separate lives, professional and private,' says Kopylova. 'We may fight a bit on the floor during practice, but when we leave the dance hall, everything is behind us. It's gone, it's forgotten.'

Kopylova danced with Aled Jones in the second series, and he couldn't find enough good things to say about her during the course of training (not surprising, really, as she helped him to lose masses of weight). Her methods had been simple, but effective: she started off by calling him 'Five Bellies' and 'Shrek', until he got the message and laid off the pies. But when they were knocked out after the semi-final, she was shocked and, by her own admission, cried for three hours after the show. She rallied quickly, however, and threw her support behind her husband. 'Please,' she asked, 'all the votes for me, just give them to Darren.' It worked.

She had another Darren on her mind in series three, of course – Darren Gough, whom she transformed from a cocky cricketer into 'the Yorkshire Valentino', according to Bruno Tonioli. This year sees Kopylova switching from cricket to rugby as she partners Wasps and England Rugby star Matt Dawson.

Ian Waite

Ian Waite's partnership with Denise Lewis enraptured the judges. 'Exotic! Sultry! Sexy!' raved Bruno – and it wasn't just Lewis's feline grace that caught his fancy.

Waite, a Latin champion since his teens, is a past master at whipping up passion on the dance floor. And it wasn't just during the competition that he brought feelings to boiling point. Sparks flew during training, too, as Waite goaded Denise Lewis into working harder. 'Do you want to be good on Saturday, or not?' he snapped. 'He has undergone some kind of metamorphosis,' complained Lewis. 'He's turned into Superbitch. I'm going to tear his head off by Wednesday.'

Fortunately for all concerned, there was no murder on the dance floor, and Waite and Lewis danced their way through to the final, where their only serious competition, was Jill Halfpenny and Darren Bennett. It was a close call – but ultimately the viewers' votes put Waite in second place. But Waite got his revenge in series three, when, as Zoe Ball's partner, he became the highest-placed male professional dancer in the show, ending up in third place. He'll be hoping to better that this year as he takes to the floor with dance diva Mica Paris.

Hazel Newberry

Like Kylie Jones in the first series, Hazel Newberry was no sooner in Strictly Come Dancing *than she was out. Hers was the misfortune to be partnered with Quentin Willson – easily the worst dancer of the 30 celebrity contestants to date, a man who made David Dickinson look like Nijinsky.*

This was hardly fair on Newberry, who's famous in the dance world for her elegance on the dance floor. She, after all, was likened by Bruno Tonioli to a Ferrari (while Willson, you will recall, was more of a Robin Reliant).

During a 12-year partnership with Christopher Hawkins, Newberry won most of the ballroom titles available to her, starting with the Open British Youth Modern Ballroom title in 1992 and never really stopping after that. They turned professional in 1997, and in 2001 and 2002 they won the British National Professional Dance Championships. Further international victories followed, and she was a natural choice for *Strictly Come Dancing*'s second series.

'The show came along at a really good time for me, after I'd just split with Christopher Hawkins,' she said. 'I'd seen the first series, and thought it was fantastic – and I knew it would be a great challenge for me.' Before the casting, Newberry had expressed her hope that she would be teamed up with a sports personality or 'someone like Paul O'Grady, someone who's game for a laugh and a total personality, willing to give it 100 per cent'. Unfortunately, this was not to be. Quentin Willson was none of those things, and he stomped them out of the competition in a lumbering Cha Cha Cha in the first week. Newberry was under no illusions.

'That routine had a few complicated steps,' she said, 'and I just thought, "Nah – this isn't going to work".'

Series Three

Zoe Ball

As a self-confessed 'idiot dancer', Zoe Ball made an amazing journey to emerge as one of the most impressive performers of the three series. And nobody was more surprised than her!

NAME Zoe Ball

DAY JOB Radio and TV presenter

DANCE PARTNER Ian Waite

BEST DANCE Three 38s, for their Tangos in week 7 and the final, and a Samba in the final.

WORST DANCE 29 for the week-three Jive.

THE JUDGES SAID Bruno: 'What a glamour puss you've turned out to be!'. Arlene: 'You sent the standard of the competition up into the stratosphere.'

HOW DID THEY DO Third place in the final.

'I'm not very feminine, and my fear is that I might end up looking like a Tweenie,' said Zoe Ball at the beginning of the third series. 'But I love dancing with the dads and uncles at weddings, because they always know what they're doing. There's something great about being flung around by a man.' The man in question was Ian Waite, who coaxed the very best out of Ball, steering her well clear of Tweenie territory. In fact, within a very short time she had emerged as one of the most graceful women on the floor, using her height and long limbs to great advantage. 'The little beach donkey has turned into a gazelle!' said Arlene Phillips – and that's a great compliment coming from her.

After an impressive opening Waltz, Ball and Waite worked hard on their technique, and seemed very much at home in each other's arms ('You should have children!' said tactless Craig Revell Horwood). Ball's newly awakened femininity shone in the costumes she wore, and her scores stayed in the high 30s nearly every week. Even the Paso Doble – stumbling block for many a celebrity dancer – got a respectable 33 points in the semi final, despite unkind remarks from the judges.

In the final, however, Ball was no match for the two surprise stars of the show, Colin Jackson and Darren Gough – and she was happy to take third place behind them. She delivered an extraordinary Tango, and left the floor with a smile on her face. 'We knew we were leaving in third place,' she said. 'Those two boys up there have improved so much.' But by the end of the series, she'd got the dance bug – and had already signed up for flamenco classes.

Darren Gough

You don't really associate the cricket pitch with the dance floor – or at least you didn't, until Darren Gough came along. The energetic, extrovert England cricket hero surprised everyone – not least himself – with his fancy footwork.

Darren Gough didn't have high expectations when he started out in *Strictly Come Dancing*. 'As a sportsman I'm naturally competitive, but I think I'm going to be rubbish. I hope my personality will win me votes – like Christopher Parker's did.' Gough's personality certainly made him popular with the viewers – but it takes more than a cheeky smile to win *Strictly Come Dancing*, and after a shaky start Gough discovered an untapped dance talent and suddenly transformed himself from a 'rhino' into a 'proud, hunky matador'.

Received wisdom was that it would be very hard for a male celebrity to win *Strictly Come Dancing* – not only would he have to learn all the steps, but he'd also have to learn how to lead. Gough, however, was a natural leader, and his rapport with Lilia Kopylova was instant. By the second week they were moving through the Quickstep with ease and grace, and from that point on their scores climbed steadily towards the final. There was a brief wobble when Gough 'went into Dalek mode', according to Bruno Tonioli, during the week-five Viennese Waltz, but they fought back in the second half of the series and made it to the final.

Before the big night, they were relaxed. 'It would be daft to say it wouldn't be nice to win,' said Gough, 'but our final is actually getting to the final'. In the event, they were the outstanding couple, and Gough impressed the judges with his ability to lead. The final scores were pretty much level-pegging with Colin and Erin – but, finally, it was Gough's combination of dance talent and personality that won the day, and the viewers crowned him king of the third series.

NAME Darren Gough
DAY JOB Cricketer
DANCE PARTNER Lilia Kopylova
BEST DANCE The Paso Doble in the final scored 36.
WORST DANCE A bad start with the first-week Cha Cha Cha, which only scored 19.
THE JUDGES SAID Bruno: 'The Yorkshire Valentino.' Arlene: 'Like watching a peacock in full regalia.'
HOW DID THEY DO Winners of series three.

Siobhan Hayes

The My Family *star didn't go into* Strictly Come Dancing *with a killer instinct. 'Everyone wants to win,' says Siobhan Hayes, 'but I'm just going to wait and see what happens.'*

'Someone has to go out in the first week,' said Siobhan Hayes just before appearing on *Strictly Come Dancing,* 'and if it's me then so be it. Such is life.' These words were prophetic, and Hayes only had time for a single Waltz with partner Matthew Cutler before being voted off the show. 'I'd like to get as far as doing the Waltz,' she'd said before the show, 'because it's so ladylike and elegant. But even though it looks easy, I'm sure it's going to be really hard to learn. If I become a good enough dancer, I might get a job in a musical. I'd love to have a go at that.'

'She'd worked hard in training', said Cutler, and even the judges admitted that she looked the part. 'She did well, she worked really hard and she took on everything I said about posture,' said Cutler. So what went wrong? 'With acting, you can stop and start and get it right,' said Hayes. 'But this was live, going out to millions of people, and that's what I was thinking on the night. That was the worry. I wanted to get through for Matthew, really. The training was the best part of the experience. We got on really well, and we just laughed all the time.'

Sadly, the Hayes–Cutler partnership was never allowed to develop, and when it came to a straight choice between Will Thorp and Siobhan Hayes, the public made its mind up against her.

NAME Siobhan Hayes
DAY JOB Actor
DANCE PARTNER Matthew Cutler
BEST/WORST DANCE 15 points for the Waltz in week one.
THE JUDGES SAID Len: 'I thought it was quite a good performance.'
HOW DID THEY DO First to leave the show in the first week.

Colin Jackson

*A stranger to the dance floor and terrified of getting 'creased',
Colin Jackson quickly turned athletic prowess into ballroom grace,
and fought his way through to the silver medal.*

Athletes have always done well on *Strictly Come Dancing*: they're physically fit, and usually have pretty good co-ordination. But Colin Jackson looked at one point as if he'd buck the trend. 'I haven't danced since I was a kid,' he said at the beginning of the series, 'and I don't even dance in nightclubs. I'm frightened of getting creased.'

Erin Boag took him in hand, though, and developed Jackson into a competent dancer by the first round. From that point onwards, Jackson just seemed to gain in confidence, and was a strong contender for the final honours. Their scores stayed in the 30s throughout the show, despite a few setbacks – not least when Jackson was called for jury service in the fourth week! Gradually he became more confident with the drama and emotion of the dances, and impressed with a sexy Samba in the fifth week and a technically excellent Viennese Waltz in week seven. Arlene Phillips even offered him a job; not bad for a dancer described early in the competition as 'Robocop'.

By the eighth week, Jackson had his eye on the crown. 'This week you had the passion and intensity of a Latin dancer,' said Bruno Tonioli. His ballroom wasn't bad either; the semi-final Waltz had the judges raving and scored 37. On the night of the final, he and Erin gave a display-standard Quickstep and a smouldering Rumba – but it wasn't quite enough to get the top prize. Their freestyle let them down (Bruno thought it 'belonged to an end-of-the-pier summer show') and they had to be content with second place.

NAME Colin Jackson
DAY JOB Olympic athlete and sports commentator
DANCE PARTNER Erin Boag
BEST DANCE Their Quickstep in the final got 39.
WORST DANCE 26 for the week-three Tango.
THE JUDGES SAID Len: 'The Welsh dragon melts the heart of the Ice Maiden'. Arlene: 'The words "trip the light fantastic" were written for Colin.'
HOW DID THEY DO Came second in the final.

Gloria Hunniford

TV legend, style icon and friend of the stars, Gloria Hunniford was a natural for Strictly Come Dancing. *But could a woman of 65 ever compete seriously against dancers less than half her age?*

NAME Gloria Hunniford
DAY JOB TV presenter
DANCE PARTNER Darren Bennett
BEST DANCE Her first-week Waltz scored 22.
WORST DANCE A disappointing 17 for the Rumba.
THE JUDGES SAID Bruno: 'The lady and the toyboy!'. Len: 'When we watch you it makes us happy.'
HOW DID THEY DO Voted off in the third week.

The first time she met her professional dance partner Darren Bennett, Gloria Hunniford said, 'It's just as well you know what it's like to win, because you won't this time.' It wasn't the most positive attitude with which to start the competition, but Hunniford just felt she was being realistic. 'How can I as an individual ever match up to someone like Colin Jackson?' she said. 'I've seen how tough the training is, and I'm just hoping that the show will make me fitter. My only worry is that my feet won't do what my brain is telling them to. I was taught to dance as a child, and I understand the fundamentals of ballroom dancing – that's where I think older contestants have an edge over the younger ones. As long as I don't fall down the stairs before I've even got on the dance floor, I should be fine.'

Bennett turned out to be the best possible teacher, and was impressed by his partner's determination. 'She's been very competitive with herself,' he said, 'and she's doing fantastically well.' Hunniford trained hard, and was delighted with the results, even when she was voted out of the show in the third week. 'It's been life-changing,' she said. 'I've had a ball and even lost a bit of weight. I've had a tough few years, and this was a really good kick-start into doing something for joy.'

Despite Hunniford's misgivings, she made a creditable start on the show, and with a little more time could have emerged as one of the surprise successes of *Strictly Come Dancing*. But the competition was hot, and her sense of rhythm let her down a little before she had a chance to shine.

James Martin

Chef James Martin didn't look like an obvious dancer, but what he lacked in natural grace he more than made up for in determination. Hard work took him all the way to the semi-final.

'I only really dance when I'm drunk,' confessed James Martin at the beginning of the third series, claiming that 'there's always alcohol involved when I get onto the dance floor.' It was a typical macho attitude towards dancing, and he'd have to break through if he was ever going to get beyond the first couple of weeks. 'I want to succeed,' he said as training began. 'I can guarantee that I'll try harder than anyone else. As a chef, I'm used to putting in the hours.' He stayed away from the pub, hit the gym and attempted to improve his physical fitness – and he'd need it. With partner Camilla Dallerup, he stayed in the show for a gruelling nine weeks.

Martin wasn't the greatest technical dancer, but he impressed the judges and viewers with his personality, and quickly established himself as something of a sex symbol. Arlene Phillips was impressed. 'You're a bit of a pudding from the waist down,' she said in the first week, 'but from the waist up, you had masses of sex appeal.' She was certainly never that charitable to the female contestants.

Martin and Dallerup's scores hovered around the high 20s for the first few weeks, before a disastrous Jive in week six knocked them right back to 20. They scraped through to the semi, knowing that it was likely to be their last appearance. They pulled off an elegant Foxtrot, and bowed out on their best score. 'I knew we were going to come bottom,' said Martin, 'so I felt I'd just go out there and really go for it.' Dallerup was as proud as could be. 'It was very important for James to hear the words "you can dance"', she said. 'If this man can make it, any man can.'

NAME James Martin
DAY JOB Chef
DANCE PARTNER Camilla Dallerup
BEST DANCE Their last dance, the Foxtrot in week eight.
WORST DANCE The Jive in week 6, and the samba in week eight, scored 20.
THE JUDGES SAID Arlene: 'You danced like a goalie.' Bruno: 'Sometimes you looked like a murderer.'
HOW DID THEY DO Knocked out in the semi-final.

Jaye Jacobs

Beautiful, charming, famous and talented – and she'd even had a spot of dance training. The Holby City star looked like a dead cert at the start of series three. So what went wrong?

Jaye Jacobs should have done better than she did. As an actor, she was used to playing a part, performing in front of millions of people on television and moving her body. She studied tap as a child, and did Dance and Drama when training as an actor, although she claimed that 'I was never any good at dancing, I was always at the bottom of the class'. But with so many advantages, and a teacher like Andrew Cuerden leading her through the training, there was every chance that she was going to be a success in *Strictly Come Dancing*.

Jaye's scores were never that bad – in her two performances, she remained above 20 – but the judges weren't impressed and, said the votes, neither were the viewers. The first-week Waltz fell a little flat, while the second (and last) dance was no improvement. 'I was so nervous in the Rumba,' she said. 'When I started off I had three steps and that was it – I literally couldn't walk.'

So is this another case of the curse of Holby General? Previous contestants from *Casualty* and *Holby City* have found *Strictly Come Dancing* just too tough to combine with their ongoing work commitments. Jacobs was confident at the start of the series that she could manage to juggle conflicting demands – but never had a chance to prove her mettle.

NAME Jaye Jacobs
DAY JOB Actor, *Holby City*
DANCE PARTNER Andrew Cuerden
BEST DANCE Their first week Waltz scored 25.
WORST DANCE The Rumba in week two.
THE JUDGES SAID Arlene: 'Get together and act the part!'. Craig: 'The dance didn't get started.'
HOW DID THEY DO Knocked out in the second week.

Dennis Taylor

The snooker legend announced at the beginning of the third series that he had 'no intention of winning', which was just as well, as his scores remained low. But his obvious effort kept him popular with the public.

'I've been dancing ever since I was a boy growing up in Ireland,' said Dennis Taylor at the start of the series, but you wouldn't have known it from his first couple of performances, which lacked technical precision and pizzazz. Izabela Hannah coached him through the Cha Cha Cha, the Quickstep and the Jive, but it wasn't enough to impress the judges. 'It was like an Emperor penguin trying to hold an egg between its legs,' said Bruno Tonioli of Taylor's Quickstep, and things didn't get much better from that point onwards.

Craig Revell Horwood turned out to be Taylor's special nemesis, describing his Paso Doble as 'absolutely woeful' and likening him to Quentin Willson in the second series. Taylor was stung, and hit back at Craig, challenging him to learn snooker to a professional standard in five days. This was not a good move, and Taylor was voted out in the fifth week, despite delivering his best-ever performance in a competent Samba. It was his posture that let him down; obviously all that time stooping over snooker tables had left its mark.

'It feels a bit strange today,' he told Claudia Winkleman after being knocked out, 'because we should have been practising today. But my feet feel a lot better. I'm going to miss the practice. It's the greatest experience I've had in my life. I was relaxed when I was practising, but on Saturday nights I was terrified. But if someone had said a few months ago that I would be dancing in front of millions of people, I would never have believed them.'

NAME Dennis Taylor
DAY JOB World-snooker champion and commentator
DANCE PARTNER Izabela Hannah
BEST DANCE Their last dance, the Samba in week five.
WORST DANCE The judges hated their week-four Paso Doble.
THE JUDGES SAID Bruno: 'Coarse and clumsy.' Len: 'I want to take a snooker cue and stick it up your shirt.'
HOW DID THEY DO Knocked out in week five.

Patsy Palmer

Walford's most famous redhead was paired with ballroom's Mr Smooth. Would it be a prize-winning partnership?

NAME Patsy Palmer
DAY JOB Actor
DANCE PARTNER Anton du Beke
BEST DANCE The Tango in week three, which scored 35.
WORST DANCE A shabby Waltz in the first week.
THE JUDGES SAID Bruno: 'Smooth, effortless and elegant.' Len: 'I was expecting Fred and Barney, but I got Fred and Ginger.'
HOW DID THEY DO Knocked out in week eight.

One of the bookies' favourites at the beginning of the third series, Patsy Palmer had all the qualities that it took to become a *Strictly Come Dancing* champion. She had relevant experience – years of dance classes as a child, professional stage experience, even her own dance-based fitness video. As if that wasn't enough, she was following in the footsteps of another ex-EastEnder, series two winner Jill Halfpenny. 'Dancing in musicals is a challenge, but there are only a few set routines for each show,' she said. 'This is going to be much harder, because there's so much to learn.'

Her fears proved to be well founded, and in her first apperance on the show, dancing a Waltz with partner Anton du Beke, she got nervous and flustered and her footwork suffered as a result. A week of hard graft in the rehearsal studio paid off, however, and by the second show the scores were up into the mid 20s as Palmer gained confidence and let her personality shine through. Technically, she couldn't compete with the likes of Colin Jackson and Zoe Ball, and occasionally her footwork was sloppy – but at her best, she was the favourite of both judges and viewers. Even Arlene Phillips was impressed, and said Palmer deserved a place in the final.

But it was not to be. Against the stiffest of competition, Palmer was voted out in the eighth show, despite a triumphant American Smooth. Du Beke hailed his partner as 'the most completely wonderful person to be with,' and Palmer, with admirable modesty, said she was just glad to have raised so much money for Children in Need.

Will Thorp

Definite heart throb potential here: as a primetime BBC star thanks to Casualty, *Will Thorp looked set to appeal to the show's sizeable straight female and gay male audience. But could he actually dance?*

'The last time I danced was at my wedding two years ago,' said Will Thorp just before hitting the rehearsal studio. 'To say I'm rusty is generous; I'm totally seized up. My wife thinks it's ridiculous, but she can't wait to see me in action.' Thorp looked like a strong contender: he was naturally athletic, and looked great in the more revealing dance costumes. But he was the first to admit that dancing wasn't his forte. 'Me and a mate used to recreate the lift from Dirty Dancing, and many's the time we've been asked to leave a club after that one.'

Thorp and his partner, Hanna Haarala, got off to a shaky start with a less-than-impressive Cha Cha Cha in the first week, scoring only 18 and actually facing elimination alongside Siobhan Hayes and Matthew Cutler. Fortunately for Thorp, the viewers' vote saved him, and he improved over the coming weeks, dancing his way to a very creditable week six. A penchant for tight-fitting tops, and a growing fondness for tanning, was transforming him into a real dancer, at least if outward appearances were anything to go by (and Arlene Phillips was certainly very keen on his torso). But, week after week, he kept ending up at the lower end of the scoring table, and even went off for a bit of hardcore training at a 'boot camp', at the suggestion of his coach. It worked – but not well enough, and he was voted off after a final Tango.

In the end, he lost out to more accomplished Patsy Palmer, and by the sound of it he wasn't sorry to leave. 'I'm looking forward to going home to my little boy and sleeping with my wife!'.

NAME Will Thorp
DAY JOB Actor
DANCE PARTNER Hanna Haarala
BEST DANCE The Foxtrot in week four scored 34.
WORST DANCE 18 points for a shaky Cha Cha Cha in the first week.
THE JUDGES SAID Craig: 'You were typecast as Woody.' Bruno: 'Instead of a torrent of passion, it was a trickle.'
HOW DID THEY DO Voted off in week six.

Fiona Phillips

Another contender for the 'Kaplinsky Effect' was Fiona Phillips, the GMTV presenter who was hoping to undergo a transformation in the arms of Brendan Cole. But it didn't quite work out that way…

Fiona Phillips was a reluctant *Strictly Come Dancing* contestant. 'I don't know why I agreed to this,' she said as soon as she was signed for series three. 'My agent put a lot of pressure on me and I kept saying no. Eventually it was my husband who convinced me.' Phillips's debut on the show wasn't promising, and even though she thought she'd be better at the dances 'where I can cling on to someone,' her Waltz failed to impress the judges, and scored only 11 points with the judges, not helped by Brendan Cole's decision to stick an illegal lift into the routine. Arlene Phillips was particularly critical, and so began another of the great *Strictly Come Dancing* stand-offs, as the two Phillipses took potshots at each other from either side of the judges' desk.

Things improved slightly over the coming weeks, and Brendan Cole managed to coax a semi-decent Foxtrot out of his partner for their fourth and final performance on the show. But it was too late, and they were soon out of the running. Phillips gamely said that she'd enjoyed her time on the show, and said that she felt there was 'a glimmer of hope' towards the end of the run. Sadly, that glimmer was extinguished.

NAME Fiona Phillips
DAY JOB *GMTV* presenter
DANCE PARTNER Brendan Cole
BEST DANCE 20 for the Foxtrot in week four.
WORST DANCE A meagre 11 for their debut Waltz.
THE JUDGES SAID Arlene: 'So awful, I don't want to say.' Craig: 'Lame, lame, lame.'
HOW DID THEY DO Knocked out in the fourth week.

Bill Turnbull

Breakfast News anchor by day, dance floor demon come Saturday night, this double life took its toll on Bill Turnbull, who ended up doing 14-hour days in order to accommodate his training.

Bill Turnbull became hooked on *Strictly Come Dancing* during the first series, watching his *Breakfast News* colleague Natasha Kaplinsky being transformed from reluctant contestant to sure-footed victor. Could lightning strike in the same place twice? 'I'm not a natural dancer,' he said at the start of the third series. 'My wife says that if I could create a sitting-down-with-beer-dance, that would be my favourite.'

Mrs T's fears proved to be ungrounded, however, as Turnbull sailed through the first week with an impressive Cha Cha Cha that even impressed Bruno Tonioli. Turnbull was delighted; his game-plan had always been to 'get through the first round, then take it week by week and try not to embarrass myself or my family too much'. Much of his success was due to partner Karen Hardy, a doyenne amongst dance teachers who came out of retirement especially for the series, and coached Turnbull from clodhopper to 'stud muffin', as she put it. The judges weren't sure; Arlene Phillips called him 'a rabbit caught in the headlights', and Craig Revell Horwood likened him to Quentin Crisp in his Paso Doble.

After a good start, things went downhill for Bill and Karen. Long days and injury were taking their toll, and despite an all-out effort for the week six Rumba (for which he had special spousal permission to be 'sexy'), the judges were getting frosty. They rallied for the week-seven Waltz, but it was too late, and they were out of the show. 'I'm glad because it was getting harder each week,' said Turnbull, 'but sad because I'm not going to dance with Karen any more. I had so much fun with the practice.'

NAME Bill Turnbull
DAY JOB Journalist, BBC *Breakfast News* presenter
DANCE PARTNER Karen Hardy
BEST DANCE Best foot forward with the Cha Cha Cha in week one, which scored 29.
WORST DANCE The Rumba in week six, a lumbering if determined performance.
THE JUDGES SAID Len: 'This man deserves a medal for work above and beyond the call of duty.'
HOW DID THEY DO A creditable seven weeks.

Andrew Cuerden

There were high hopes for Andrew Cuerden, a hugely talented South African dancer who specializes in the Paso Doble – but with only two weeks in the show, he never had the chance to shine.

It's impossible not to feel sorry for the professional dancers who get knocked out early in the competition; through no fault of their own (usually), they're unable to show the viewing public just how great they are. So when Jaye Jacobs was voted off the show in the second week, she was far more concerned for Andrew Cuerden than she was for herself. What went wrong? 'I don't think we were the worst,' said Cuerden, 'but I think we fell through the crack of not being bad enough so people felt sorry for us. And we weren't good enough to get the marks from the judges.'

Whatever the reasons, the disappointing result left Cuerden hungry for more. 'I've enjoyed the whole experience, and just feel sad that we haven't been able to show our full potential. We never really got stuck in.'

One of the many talented dancers to come from southern Africa to compete in the UK, Andrew Cuerden grew up in Zimbabwe and took his first tentative steps onto the dance floor at his older sister's 21st birthday party. 'I was eight years old, painfully shy and self-conscious, and wild horses could not have pulled me onto a dance floor. But my sister, the party animal of the family, dragged me on and gave me my first informal dance lesson. I then asked everyone at the party to dance and didn't stop until four in the morning.' Cuerden took up dance lessons in his teens, alternating it with rugby matches at the weekends. 'My girlfriends from dancing used to come and support me at rugby, so my team mates soon got jealous that I was getting the babes and they weren't!' Eventually, he had to make a choice between his two favourite pastimes – he opted to pursue dancing, competing for seven years in South Africa before moving to England in the mid-90s.

He started *Strictly Come Dancing* in confident mood. 'Celebrities are just people; they're beginners – and I'm used to dealing with beginners on a daily basis. The only difference will be that there's a camera in the room.' After he was knocked out he had the satisfaction of watching his dance partner Hanna Haarala clocking up a respectable six weeks with Will Thorp.

Hanna Haarala

Millions of Strictly Come Dancing *viewers would love to have been in Hanna Haarala's shoes, waltzing around the studio floor with* Casualty *heart-throb Will Thorp. For her, however, it was just another job.*

Finnish dancer Hanna Haarala was the first to admit that she didn't have the faintest idea who any of the celebrity contestants were. However, as soon as she got her hands on Will Thorp, she became determined to get him as far as possible in the competition, even if that meant sending him for a bit of special bootcamp training to toughen him up for the later rounds.

Hard work holds no fear for Haarala, who has been dancing competitively since her teens. She was unwilling to get too involved with dancing in her childhood; she was already a keen skater, and that was where she saw her future. 'At my first dance class at the age of ten, I said, "I will not stop ice-skating because of dancing." Three months later, that's exactly what I did.'

Throughout her teens in her native Finland, Haarala worked her way through the competitive circuit and started teaching as well. With her partner, Mikko Kaasalainen, she represented Finland at the European and World Games, before dissolving the partnership after three years. That's when Andrew Cuerden stepped in, calling her up with a view to a try-out and flying to Finland to meet her. 'I liked his personality and I thought it would be good for me to move to London and learn more about dancing. It all happened really quickly. He flew to Finland for a trial, I flew to London for a trial and we decided after one lesson to form a partnership.' The Haarala–Cuerden partnership doesn't extend beyond the dance floor, though; she has a boyfriend, Joe, tucked away at home.

With Will Thorp, she managed a creditable six weeks in the competition, before being voted out after an underwhelming stab at the Tango. Craig Revell Horwood described it as 'absolute rubbish', which may have been a little uncharitable, but there was certainly a sense that she'd taken him as far as he was going to go.

Izabela Hannah

Like many a young girl before her, Izabela Hannah was lured into dance classes by seeing Patrick Swayze in Dirty Dancing *at an impressionable age. And then came Dennis Taylor…*

Before starting training for series three, Izabela Hannah was full of enthusiasm. 'The key to my teaching is passion and excitement,' she said, 'because that's what I always feel when I dance. When people come to my studio for classes they say that's what I give them. Hopefully, that will happen with Dennis. I am a very passionate person, and I know I can use that to push him a little bit further. I just hope I get

enthusiasm and commitment in return.'

Perhaps, being Polish and having lived in America for the last few years, she didn't know that Dennis Taylor, and British snooker players in general, are not exactly a byword for 'passion and excitement'. She'd grown up on dreams of *Dirty Dancing*, and persuaded her parents to take her to dance school as a direct result of seeing the film.

'I learned everything from disco to Rumba,' she says. 'It was easy for me to commit to dance, because I loved it so much.' With her teacher and husband Stephen Hannah, who retired from competition in 2000, she was part of one of the most exciting teams in the ballroom world. But working with celebrities is a different matter altogether. Dennis Taylor tried hard, put in the training, but just couldn't sort out his problems with posture and footwork, and the couple were out of the show after five weeks. Hannah didn't mind, though – she admitted that she'd fallen for Dennis Taylor's charms, and thoroughly enjoyed her time in the competition. 'We went out on our highest score, and that showed how much he'd improved. I just think that after all that, it was a little bit disappointing to be voted off.'

Matthew Cutler

Joining the list of 'one-hit wonders' to grace the Strictly Come Dancing *studio is Matthew Cutler, whose partnership with Siobhan Hayes just never got off the ground.*

Of all the new dancers to appear in the third series of *Strictly Come Dancing*, Matthew Cutler should have had the biggest advantage: his former wife and professional partner, Nicole Cutler, appeared in series two. However, there's no whiff of nepotism here: Mr Cutler won the British and UK Closed Professional Latin Championships last year, and the World and European Championships this year, as well as gaining a cupboard full of other trophies since he started dancing at the age of ten. The Cutlers split in 2003; he now dances with Danish champion, Charlotte Engstrand.

He describes his dance style as 'sensual and sexy. I don't like the gymnastic style where the priority is trick steps and things like that. I can really get into the Jive, as it's a relaxed dance and not too controlled and restricted.' But would he be able to relax with a celebrity in his arms – possibly one who isn't a natural dancer? 'I don't really mind who I teach as long as she is willing to learn and not worried about making a fool of herself. It's so draining when you're trying to teach someone and they don't really want to learn.'

And how did he feel about taking on fellow professionals and rivals like Darren Bennett and Anton du Beke? 'I'm quite competitive, and I hate to lose. I'd rather not take part in something if I knew that I wasn't going to have a good chance of winning,

whether it's tennis, or running, or stupid things like arm-wrestling in the pub.'

But that was before he met Siobhan Hayes, whose heart just never seemed to be in the competition. 'It's not nice being the first out,' he said. 'It would have been nice to stay in a bit longer, so that we could get used to it and maybe do a bit of Latin. I'm a little bit gutted. I know the judges are there to criticise, but all they did was point out the things that were wrong.' Better luck this year, Matthew: he's partnering Carol Smillie in series four.

Karen Hardy

Latin-American legend Karen Hardy came out of retirement specially to appear on Strictly Come Dancing. *After six years out of competitive dancing, was she up to the challenge of Bill Turnbull?*

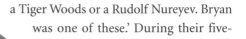

She was the former Latin world champion – he was the *Breakfast News* presenter. Coming from two such different worlds, could they make magic on the dancefloor? If anyone could lick Bill Turnbull into shape, it was Karen Hardy, a name spoken with reverence in Latin-American circles. With her professional partner Bryan Watson – a former World, International, European, United Kingdom and British Amateur Latin Champion – she was at the very top of the profession throughout the 90s. Hardy was already a very experienced competitive dancer – but Watson was 'a god. In every form of art or sport, there's someone who comes along and is a phenomenon – a Tiger Woods or a Rudolf Nureyev. Bryan was one of these.' During their five-year partnership they represented England all over the world, and became one of the most respected partnerships. She retired in 1999, but not before they had been credited with breaking the mould of Latin-American dancing, and dragging the dance form into the 21st century. 'To create a step and then see it copied around the world is an indescribable reward. They don't come any more dedicated and focused than Bryan, and that's why we were able to break the rules that had been set in stone for so long.'

But Bill Turnbull was not Bryan Watson, and despite Hardy's best efforts their partnership never really took off. When they Tangoed to 'Perhaps' in week three, Craig Revell Horwood decided, 'I would have to say "perhaps not". It was all very camp and passive.' Arlene Phillips dismissed their Paso Doble as 'common'. Amazingly, Hardy managed to get Turnbull back week after week, and they survived until show seven. Hardy had no regrets. 'It was the greatest thing I've ever done,' she said. The final result delighted her. 'Darren Gough was a real man's man on the dancefloor. He basically said "guys, it's cool, you can have fun". That's a great example to set.' This year, Hardy's got her hands on another cricket star, Mark Ramprakash.

The Dances

Rumba

From Africa, via Cuba to America, the Rumba is the number that burns up the dance floor with an irresistible mixture of sexual passion and rhythm.

The Rumba is a romantic dance; it tells the story of seduction between a man and a woman. They flirt, then there's attraction. The woman then tries to get away, but the man pulls her back. It's the only slow Latin-American dance – and rhythm is all. The couple has to be connected, disciplined and always showing the right kind of lines. It's one of the hardest dances for a beginner to master – but in the hands of the professionals, the Rumba is one of the sexiest performances on the dance floor. Here Darren Bennett and Lilia Kopylova demonstrate the classic Rumba positions.

History

The Rumba has always had a slightly risqué reputation in dance circles. Its origins are ancient, going back to African ritual dances that were transported to the New World by the slave trade. It surfaced in its modern form in Cuba in the 1890s, when it was repressed by the authorities for its 'lewdness' and overt sexual overtones. A sanitized version was popularized in America in the 1930s, where it spread rapidly due to the popularity of songs such as 'The Peanut Vendor'. It retains core elements of sexual teasing and female domination; essentially, it's a dance of seduction.

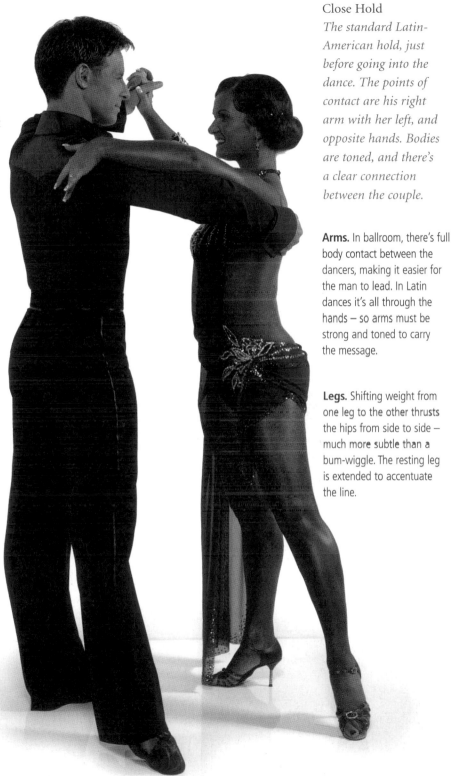

Make-up. Like all Latin dances, skin and hair tones tend to be dark, with smoky eyes for the women. Lilia's hair is worn up, in a style that evokes the nightclubs of the 1930s and 40s.

Dress. A simple black silhouette for Darren, to accentuate the line of the dance. Women's Rumba dresses are often cut away and revealing, to accentuate the sexual nature of the dance of seduction.

Posture. The Rumba is all based around the classic Latin-American hold but, as it progresses, the dancers' bodies will be alternately erect and sinuous.

Feet. Feet remain toned at all times throughout the Rumba. Although it's a slow dance, the dancers must maintain a disciplined line that 'follows through' the extremities.

Close Hold
The standard Latin-American hold, just before going into the dance. The points of contact are his right arm with her left, and opposite hands. Bodies are toned, and there's a clear connection between the couple.

Arms. In ballroom, there's full body contact between the dancers, making it easier for the man to lead. In Latin dances it's all through the hands – so arms must be strong and toned to carry the message.

Legs. Shifting weight from one leg to the other thrusts the hips from side to side – much more subtle than a bum-wiggle. The resting leg is extended to accentuate the line.

What we're looking for in the Rumba is a connection between the couple. When Darren and Lilia dance the Rumba, they're looking at each other nearly all the time – and you can see the connection through their arms and hands, the slightest pressure and she's spinning round. It's all about that contact. Look at the basic hold, and you'll see that, although they're barely touching, they're still communicating. The Rumba should be romantic rather than sexy; it's all about seduction and courtship. The man might be leading, but if you look at the basic hold you see that in the Rumba, as in life, the girl always has the upper hand.

Fan Position

A basic Rumba step, showing how the man leads through the simplest of hand connections. The couple step apart, finishing at right angles to one another.

Opening Out

A variation moving the position of the couple from left to right. Her foot comes in front of his foot as they move from side to side.

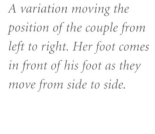

Sliding Doors

An advanced version of a basic Rumba step. The line is almost symmetrical – but he's on his forward foot, she's on the back foot. The couple will then cross positions to the other side.

◑ Rope Spin

The man supports the woman with his right arm while she spins on the balls of her feet and turns. The feet are crossed, one in front of the other, before she whips round in a spiral move.

◑ Romance

A typical Rumba pose or 'line', showing the romance of the dance, with the woman's head resting on the man's chest, his hand caressing her neck. Despite the mood, limbs remain toned at all times.

◑ Rumba Drop

One of the most spectacular moments in the Rumba, and a guaranteed crowd-pleaser. Despite the abandon of the pose, the line remains correct from the tips of fingers to the end of toes.

◑ Rumba Line

Sometimes the Rumba can get pretty athletic. In this typical rumba line the man holds the woman by hooking her leg around his waist.

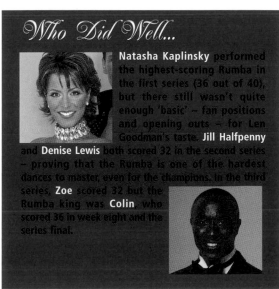

Who Did Well...

Natasha Kaplinsky performed the highest-scoring Rumba in the first series (36 out of 40), but there still wasn't quite enough 'basic' – fan positions and opening outs – for Len Goodman's taste. **Jill Halfpenny** and **Denise Lewis** both scored 32 in the second series – proving that the Rumba is one of the hardest dances to master, even for the champions. In the third series, **Zoe** scored 32 but the Rumba king was **Colin**, who scored 36 in week eight and the series final.

Waltz

The epitome of elegance, the Waltz is the dance that most people think characterizes ballroom dancing. But the shuffling of amateurs demonstrates that it is more complicated than it appears.

The Waltz, of course, is danced in 3:4 time – hence the rhythmical rise and fall of the movement that's made it a ballroom favourite for 200 years. The communication between the couple is so intense in the Waltz that they should move almost as one, never breaking the contact that forms the classic ballroom hold. It's that high degree of touching that made the Waltz such a controversial dance in Victorian England, and which means it's still one of the most popular social dances in the world. Anton du Beke and Erin Boag demonstrate a dance that looks simple when it is done properly, but in reality is anything but…

History

Nowadays it's the epitome of elegant, old-fashioned ballroom dancing, but time was when the Waltz was regarded as scandalous and overtly sexual. Derived from the *volta*, a French peasant dance, it became popular in Vienna in the 18th century, spreading rapidly across Europe. When it reached England, it was immediately denounced in polite society for its excessive physical contact (social dances had hitherto kept partners at a decent arm's length). When the Prince Regent included it in a ball he held in 1816, *The Times* described the Waltz as 'the indecent foreign dance… an obscene display. We feel it a duty to warn every parent against exposing his daughter to so fatal a contagion.' Needless to say, it rapidly caught on.

Throwaway Oversway
A classic Waltz line. The man dances the woman round in front of him (small picture, left) before turning her and allowing her torso to extend back (main picture).

Make-up. The overall look for ballroom dances is less dramatic than the Latin section, however, it is more elegant. In this photo Erin wears her hair loose for a free, flowing look (although it took hours to sew in the hair extensions) and her make-up is simple and natural.

Dress. Classic white tie and tails for the man, of course: that's the uniform for nearly all ballroom. The woman wears a light and floating dress that moves with her and accentuates her rhythm.

Arms. The arms must be kept in the correct ballroom hold (see next page) whatever position the dancers adopt.

Feet. The dancers rise and fall throughout the Waltz by coming up on to the balls of their feet, turning and stepping in the classic one-two-three rhythm of the music.

Legs. Symmetry is important, and so the positions of the partners' legs frequently mirror each other. The supporting leg, concealed by the elegance of the movement, is rock solid.

Posture. No matter what variations the dancers perform, the basic hold remains solid throughout the dance.

⊘ ⊙ Ballroom Hold *(left and below) The dancers are not square on; the woman is slightly to the man's right. He places his right hand on the woman's back near the shoulder blade; her left hand rests on his right upper arm.*

↗ Whisk

The dancers' feet end in a crossed position and the bodies and heads are in a position known as promenade position.

Natural Turn

'Natural' indicates a movement going to the right ('reverse' is to the left), commencing with the man's right foot. Body contact remains constant throughout, with no space between the hips.

Left Whisk

The man remains cool and controlled while the woman is turned through the full range of the whisk movement. Again, the strength of the supporting legs is concealed by the elegance of the turn.

Promenade

A basic forward ballroom movement. The couple moves around the floor while maintaining the all-important body contact.

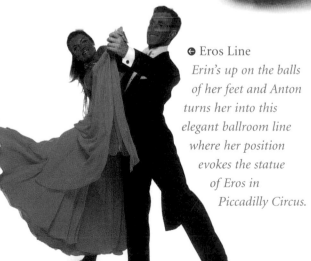

Eros Line

Erin's up on the balls of her feet and Anton turns her into this elegant ballroom line where her position evokes the statue of Eros in Piccadilly Circus.

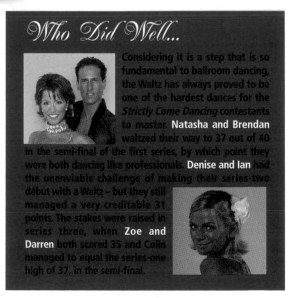

Who Did Well...

Considering it is a step that is so fundamental to ballroom dancing, the Waltz has always proved to be one of the hardest dances for the *Strictly Come Dancing* contestants to master. **Natasha and Brendan** waltzed their way to 37 out of 40 in the semi-final of the first series, by which point they were both dancing like professionals. **Denise and Ian** had the unenviable challenge of making their series-two début with a Waltz – but they still managed a very creditable 31 points. The stakes were raised in series three, when **Zoe and Darren** both scored 35 and Colin managed to equal the series-one high of 37, in the semi-final.

Paso Doble

In the ultimate expression of machismo, in this Spanish dance the man plays the role of the fearless matador, while the woman plays the cape and every other supporting role...

The melodramatic Paso Doble is one of the biggest challenges to the *Strictly Come Dancing* contestants. It's a deadly serious dance, charged with passion and violence – but, if it goes wrong, it can turn into low comedy. Even Lesley Garrett described it as 'a very silly dance', and images of Christopher Parker's bizarre interpretation of the Paso Doble are still burned on the memory. So how do the experts manage to make it work? Darren and Lilia, who are probably the best in the business, put the would-be bullfighters through their paces.

History

Unlike the rest of the Latin dances, the Paso Doble does not have its roots in Africa; this one comes directly from Spain. It's a stylized representation of the bullfight, with the man playing the part of the macho matador, the woman variously standing in for the bull, the cape, another matador or a dancer. The dance (*paso doble* means 'two step') is based on the march music at the beginning of the *corrida*, progressing to the passes between bull and fighter, and moving towards the kill. This most dramatic and narrative of dances first became popular outside Spain during the 1930s, when it swept France and ultimately the entire ballroom-dancing world.

Make-up. The Paso Doble must evoke the *corrida*, and so anything that adds to the Spanish vibe is useful. Black and red are the favoured colours – so Lilia favours dark eyes and dark lips, and accentuates her black curls with a huge red flower.

Arms. Arms and hands are constantly toned and flexed in the Paso Doble, emphasising the strength of the man and the suppleness of the woman. The flamenco feel extends through to the tips of the fingers.

Legs. A high degree of flexibility is necessary to carry off the Paso Doble properly. Both partners have to bend into extreme stretches, requiring a full range of mobility in their quadriceps and hamstrings.

Feet. The feet are used as a storytelling device in the Paso Doble: they are used to attract the bull's attention. As in all Latin dances, they remain strong and toned throughout.

⊘ Male Dominance
The man acts the part of the bullfighter in the Paso Doble, and all of his moves should accentuate his mastery of the situation. The woman is mostly the bullfighter's cape – as in this posture – bowing backwards.

Dress. Again, the mood is theatrically Spanish. Darren wears a stylized version of a bullfighter's bolero, black trimmed in red, while Lilia picks up the same colours in a flamenco-styled outfit with a tight bodice and full skirt.

Posture. Dramatic, exaggerated movements in the Paso Doble are accentuated by toned bodies flexing through the spine.

It's all about the focus and faces. You have to take this dance seriously and do it with commitment, otherwise it's not worth bothering. I look for good posture from the man, toned to the tips of his fingers, and for big dramatic shapes from the woman. They have to keep tight control in the basic steps, but go for the big effect in the attitudes (the lines they create). And they must look the part. It's no good going into a Paso Doble with a big smile. I want to see them looking angry – aggressive even. The eyes should always be focused, either on each other, on a judge, or even on a member of the audience. They must maintain that intensity right through the dance.

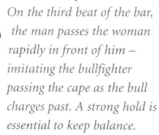

⊘ Chassé Cape
On the third beat of the bar, the man passes the woman rapidly in front of him – imitating the bullfighter passing the cape as the bull charges past. A strong hold is essential to keep balance.

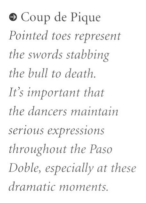

➔ Coup de Pique
Pointed toes represent the swords stabbing the bull to death. It's important that the dancers maintain serious expressions throughout the Paso Doble, especially at these dramatic moments.

⬆ Matador Throws Cape
A typical Paso Doble line. The bullfighter tosses the cape disdainfully to the ground. Lilia uses her skirt to represent the cape's cloth, while Darren maintains the severe, erect line of the bullfighter.

Role Reversal

Sometimes the bull gets the upper hand – but the bullfighter shows his mastery of the situation by dropping down to demonstrate that he isn't impressed.

Elevations

A bit of all-important basic in the Paso Doble. Elevations are a series of small side steps, up on the balls of the feet – the bodies arch and the faces look down towards the floor.

Twist Turn

Once again, the woman is the cape being worked by the bullfighter. He puts his weight on his back leg, then she comes around in front of him and they turn on the balls of their feet.

Flamenco Checks

A typical flamenco move that's been incorporated into the Paso Doble. The couple dance in front of each other in a series of flexed leg movements going from right to left, working up an intensity as the moves continue.

Who Did Well...

For some of the couples, the Paso Doble was one dance too far; they couldn't master the steps or the attitude. But it also brought out some of the best performances of the whole show. **Jill and Darren** scored 37 in the second series semi-final, with **Denise and Ian** only one point behind them. **Natasha and Brendan** were the best Paso dancers in the first series, scoring 35 out of 40. **Darren** grabbed the bull by the horns in series three, with an amazing 34 for his first Paso Doble and 36 in the final.

Foxtrot

The Foxtrot is the most elegant and graceful of ballroom dances, which evokes images of Fred Astaire and Ginger Rogers and the ballroom dance floors of the 1930s.

The slow Foxtrot is every ballroom professional's favourite dance – an elegant, gliding, sophisticated number. As in all ballroom dances, however, complex technique is masked with an illusion of ease and grace (not least for the woman, who, in the immortal words of Ginger, has to do everything the man does but 'backwards and in heels'). It's founded on the basic ballroom hold (see p.136), around which is built a routine of turns and lines, the timing varying between slow and fast. At its simplest, the Foxtrot is a combination of walks and chassés, but in the hands of Anton and Erin it is a dazzling display of technique.

History

Back in 1914, at the height of the ragtime craze, American vaudeville performer Harry Fox was having difficulty finding women to partner him in a complicated two-step routine. As a result, he added slower steps, creating the slow-quick-quick-slow rhythm that the dance has today – and people started copying him. Before long, revellers at the *Jardin de Danse* nightclub – situated above the theatre where Fox was performing – started doing their own versions of 'Fox's Trot'. It was picked up by dance stars Vernon and Irene Castle, who incorporated it into their act and made it the epitome of ballroom grace and style that it remained through countless Astaire–Rogers films.

Oversway into Aerial Ronde
The man holds the woman in the classic ballroom oversway (see p.135, and small picture, top left) before turning her quickly in front of him. She finishes with one leg raised, hence 'aerial'.

Make-up. Think Hollywood, think understated glamour, think 1930s nightclubs, and you've got an idea of the Foxtrot style.

Arms. The classic ballroom hold leads the dancers through every permutation of the Foxtrot, allowing the man to communicate perfectly through his arms and hands with his partner.

Legs. In the simple version, the legs are more or less just stepping the couple around the floor. But as the Foxtrot becomes more complicated, the legs have to be precisely placed in order to achieve accurate turns.

Dress. As with the Waltz, the dress is elegant and flowing and the man is in ballroom tails.

Posture. A loose, carefree feel is essential to the Foxtrot, with the partners mirroring each other's movements as they spin and glide across the floor.

Feet. The Foxtrot requires the dancers to shift constantly from the ball to the heel of the foot – turning on the balls and pivoting on the heels. One of the hardest ballroom techniques.

● Feather Step

The feather step – so-called because of the gentle curving shape formed by the foot – is a basic step of the Foxtrot. The man steps outside the woman on her right side on steps two and three.

● ● Heel Turns

The woman turns on her heels – a very difficult step – so the man must keep perfect balance for both of them. In this sequence, Anton and Erin prepare for the turn, then he steps across her, she puts her feet together and pivots on her heels. Then they come out of the turn.

⊙ Fallaway
His left leg is back, her right leg is forward, and they allow their upper bodies to fall away from each other while maintaining the correct ballroom body contact throughout.

⊙ Same-foot Lunge
A perfect example of how the couple's legs mirror each other through the Foxtrot – they both take their weight on to the same leg. Anton holds Erin in an oversway while their feet point out in the same direction, extending the line.

⊘ Hover Cross
Another bit of basic. The man steps outside the woman on her left side, and maintains body contact.

Who Did Well...

Not surprisingly, this deceptively difficult dance was a big challenge for the less gifted hoofers. **Natasha and Brendan** got the top mark in the first series – 35 out of 40 – but they were only a single point ahead of **Lesley and Anton** who showed real aptitude for the gliding, free-and-easy style. In the second series, only the eventual winners **Jill and Darren** could approach that standard, gaining 34 out of 40 points. In series three, **Zoe and Darren** both hit an all-time Foxtrot high with 36.

Jive

The closest thing to 'modern' dances on the night club dance floor, the Jive's origins are many and varied, making this a lively, fast and contemporary form of ballroom dancing.

It couldn't be further from the passion of the Paso Doble or the romance of the Rumba. The Jive is the light, bright, contemporary dance in the Latin-American canon, and it gives the dancers a chance to show off a much wider variety of moves, drawn from dozens of different traditions. The Jive may have solidified in the 40s and 50s with elements of the lindy hop and the jitterbug, but it continues to develop with greater freedom than any other dance. It's closer in nature to the social dancing that we're used to today – which might explain why some contestants felt they could take liberties with it that the judges didn't like!

History

The exact origins of the Jive are obscure: some say it's based on Seminole Indian dances, others that it derives, like so many Latin dances, from steps performed by African slaves in the New World. By the 1880s, a form of Jive was danced competitively in the southern states of the USA – but it wasn't until the jazz-crazed 1920s that the Jive became the official youth dance of America. With its quick movements and spins, it was frowned on by older, more traditional dancers. GIs brought the Jive to Europe in the 40s, where it was considered a 'corrupting influence' (just like the Waltz, over 100 years earlier). During the 50s, it mutated into swing, boogie-woogie, jitterbugging and rock 'n' roll.

Make-up. The Jive is an informal party dance, and so the hair and make-up should give a celebratory, slightly cheeky feel. Lilia's hair is up loosely on one side – but it has to be sufficiently set so it won't whip around her face too much.

 Hitch

A typical Jive move, showing the cheeky, celebratory nature of the dance. Arms extend in perfect lines front and back, while strong, precise leg movements provide lateral symmetry.

Arms. Arms are loose and expressive (although they shouldn't just be waved around any-old-how, as some contestants have tried). Postures and lines extend right through to the fingers.

Dress. The Jive wardrobe's eclectic roots. Darren's wearing a 50s-style purple jacket – very rock 'n' roll – while Lilia's matching dress is redolent of the 1920s and 30s with its bead fringing.

Legs. Kicks from the hip, and flicks from the knee, make up many of the Jive's basic movements. The leg positions are often symmetrical, as here.

Feet. Fancy footwork is the name of the game in the Jive. The feet turn outwards into the chicken walk – or flick from the ankle – but all movements should be precise and completed.

Posture. Far less rigid and erect than in other Latin dances, the body posture in the Jive must adapt to any of the athletic moves incorporated into the routine.

◕ Kicks and Flicks

The legs are held straight and strong as they're kicked out from the hip (as here) or from the knee (into a flick).

➔ Jive Pose

Unlike a lot of dances, the Jive allows a great degree of variation between the man's and woman's role. This is a typical Jive pose, neither doing the same steps nor shadowing the other.

⊕ Chicken Walks

A basic Jive step, in which the man uses a strong hip action while the woman moves towards him with her feet turned outwards. Lilia leans right back through her spine while Darren supports her with his hand.

Jump On
This is a typical rock'n'roll move that's often incorporated into Jive performances – but it would not be allowed in competition, when the woman's feet must not both leave the ground.

Jive Pivots
A continuous circling movement as the dancers turn round and round with a variety of arm positions throughout.

Stop-and-Go
The woman comes from the man's left, he stops her and returns her, making a yo-yo movement that's familiar on rock 'n' roll dance floors.

Back Rock
This is the basic Jive step – the first thing you would learn if you went to Jive classes. Transferring the weight on to the back foot in small, quick movements allows for a full variety of turns.

Who Did Well...

Jill and Darren became the first couple ever to score a perfect 40 for their Jive on *Strictly Come Dancing*. That was way ahead of the standard of the first series, in which nobody got above **Lesley and Anton's** creditable 29. The standard crept back up – but only to 30 – for **Darren and Colin** in series three.

Ballroom Tango

Despite the salubrious origins of the dance, the aggressive yet sexy Tango is full of Latin passion and stirs up real excitement when danced with the control and power it demands.

The Tango brings a touch of Latin passion into the ballroom world – and it's a much more serious business than the frothy Foxtrot or the whirling Waltz. The lines are more rigid and severe and the movement staccato; it is more stop-and-go than the fluid sequences that are better known to ballroom dancers. Slow deliberate 'stalking' walks are alternated with sudden, fast action, which gives the dance its light and shade. It's been a tough nut to crack for the contestants on *Strictly Come Dancing*; if you don't have a natural sense of rhythm, you're never going to get the hang of the Ballroom Tango.

History

Emerging from the black ghettos of Argentina in the 1890s, the Tango originated as a dance enacting the relationship between a prostitute and her client or between an unwilling woman and a smelly gaucho. The man's flexed-knee posture recalls the stiff-legged walk of the gauchos in their leather chaps; the woman's stance, head held back, allegedly derives from the fact that most of the men hadn't washed after a day on the range. **In the prostitute and client story, her right hand, low on his hip, is supposed to be fishing for his wallet. Argentinian bands and dancers took the Tango to Europe in the 20th century, where it was cleaned up and became a pre-War craze – although it never lost its shady reputation.**

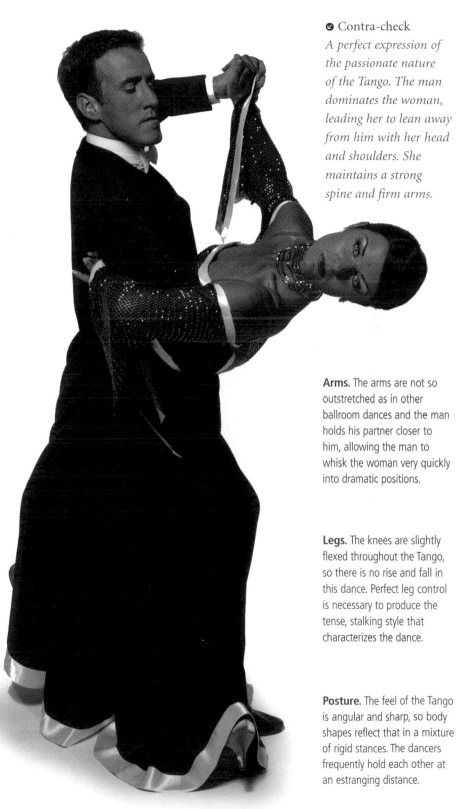

Make-up. The Tango is the most severe of all the dances, so hair tends to be scraped back off the women's faces, aiming for a high-gloss, painted-on look. The make-up is stark and dramatic.

Dress. Anton has changed his usual tails for something a little more loungey – a shorter jacket that reminds us of the Tango's informal roots. Erin completes her look with dramatic black and silver satin.

Feet. In the Tango, the feet perform a lot of different moves – they drag across the floor, they flash and stab out into the air, they fly around in fast-paced changes or cruise through slow stalks.

⊘ Contra-check
A perfect expression of the passionate nature of the Tango. The man dominates the woman, leading her to lean away from him with her head and shoulders. She maintains a strong spine and firm arms.

Arms. The arms are not so outstretched as in other ballroom dances and the man holds his partner closer to him, allowing the man to whisk the woman very quickly into dramatic positions.

Legs. The knees are slightly flexed throughout the Tango, so there is no rise and fall in this dance. Perfect leg control is necessary to produce the tense, stalking style that characterizes the dance.

Posture. The feel of the Tango is angular and sharp, so body shapes reflect that in a mixture of rigid stances. The dancers frequently hold each other at an estranging distance.

Len Says...

The Tango is an aggressive dance. There's not much smiling, but there's a lot of sex. At its best, the man should look like a raunchy gigolo who's quite capable of bending the woman over a table. Don't forget that it has its roots in a dance performed by Argentinian gauchos and prostitutes. While the Waltz and the Foxtrot are gliding dances, the Tango is flat and staccato, with sharp foot and head movements performed at lightning speed. Most dances are soft and rhythmic, but the Tango is very different and goes in big blips, like a heart monitor on a screen. It can be ugly if you do it badly, but done properly it's tremendously exciting.

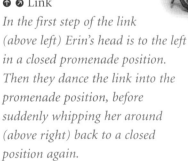

◒ ◓ Tango Hold

This differs from the basic ballroom hold. It's much tighter, his right arm is further round her body, and his left arm is closer to his body, pulling her inwards. Her left hand is further down, underneath his armpit.

↑ ↗ Link

In the first step of the link (above left) Erin's head is to the left in a closed promenade position. Then they dance the link into the promenade position, before suddenly whipping her around (above right) back to a closed position again.

⊙ Stalking Walks
Elongated steps commenced on the outside edge of the foot take the dancers across the floor. The taut attitude of the bodies and the stern facial expressions are an important part of the Tango.

⊙ Spanish Drag
The woman starts in a deep line, as the man slowly brings her up, then a little further up, before suddenly they both drop and turn into promenade position to continue their progress across the floor.

⊙ Swivel
There are many swivelling moves in the Tango, as the dancers turn on their feet and bring the other (lifted) foot round into a promenade position.

Who Did Well...

Claire and John pulled off the best Tango of the first series in the third week – but it wasn't enough to keep them in the competition. They scored 34 out of 40, putting them three points ahead of the eventual winners, Natasha and Brendan. In the second series, **Denise and Ian** were way ahead of all the competition, managing to score 35 points – that's six more than **Jill and Darren**. The series-three Tango high went to **Zoe** who managed to score 38 both in week eight and the final.

Cha Cha Cha

As the name suggests, the Cha Cha Cha is a little number that allows the dancers a bit of fun and a lot of flirting.
But if you want to win, you have to watch those illegal moves...

The Cha Cha Cha is the cheeky younger cousin of the Rumba. They share similar step patterns, but the mood could not be more different. The Rumba is all about seduction – but the Cha Cha Cha is a fun, light-hearted dance in which the couple are expressing their delight in each other's company. The woman wiggles against the man, there's lots of hip action, even a little bit of bump and grind. But, for all that, there are strict rules. No matter how exciting the dance, some holds are just plain illegal – as Paul Killick was reminded when he swept Verona Joseph off her feet in the first-ever show, and was marked down accordingly.

History

During the 1940s, everyone was dancing the mambo – or at least having a go, as it was hard and fast and difficult to perfect. Orchestras started slowing the music down, and a new dance – a modified Rumba – was introduced to go with the easier pace. There's some debate about the origin of the name: some say it's a Haitian word for a bell-like musical instrument, others that it represents the sound of sandals slapping against the floor, as danced in Cuba. The Cha Cha Cha (or Cha Cha) as danced today was formulated by the dancers Pierre and Lavelle, who introduced the triple step that differentiates it from the Rumba.

Make-up. It's a Latin dance, so, of course, dark hair and tans are the order of the day. The hair is chic and simple, though, and the make-up softer than the more dramatic dances. Sparkly accessories add to the fun mood.

Dress. 'What aren't you wearing?' asked Bruce on more than one occasion, as the women's Cha Cha Cha dresses got shorter and smaller and more revealing. Sparkle and fringing adds to the sense of speed.

Feet. Feet are turned out and show a strong shape throughout the dance, rooting the couple to the floor whatever variations they go into.

Posture. Looser and more funky than most of the Latin dances, the Cha Cha Cha allows for a full range of postures and positions.

⊘ Cuban Break
This is the second position of the Cuban break, a group of syncopated steps in which the dancers cross repeatedly in front of each other. The mood is light but sexy, even raunchy, with lots of hip action.

Arms. Lots of scope for movement with arms in the Cha Cha Cha, but the judges will always be looking for strong toning and a good finish in the fingers.

Legs. Leg lines between the two dancers are often parallel, forming some of the dance's most characteristic shapes. Toes are turned out, and there's a lot of hip action, shifting the weight from one foot to the other.

Cuban Break

As the dancers move around each other through the crossing sequence of the Cuban break, their legs remain parallel, the toes turned out. The arms are free and expressive.

New York

Cha Cha Cha originators Pierre and Lavelle discovered this move in the clubs of New York. The feet are turned out, and there's a strong 'V' shape through the bodies and outstretched arms.

Open Hip Twist

The dancers prepare to go into the Hip Twist. Darren's weight is on the front leg, Lilia's is on the back as she prepares to 'twist' round into the first part of the rotation.

◐ Aerial Rondé

Like the rondé in the Foxtrot, this is a circling movement of the leg. Beginners are encouraged to keep the rondé low and close to the floor. As dancers become more advanced, the leg moves higher.

◑ Fan

Here the Cha Cha Cha shows its closeness to the Rumba, but the attitude is perkier and cheekier.

◐ Wiggle

A typically cheeky Cha Cha Cha movement. The man's position is strong and macho, while the woman crouches at his feet, holds on to his hips and then wiggles her way up his legs.

Who Did Well...

Despite breaking the rules to such dramatic effect in the first-ever show, **Verona and Paul** got one of the best scores for the Cha Cha Cha in the first series – 27 out of 40. It wasn't a high-scoring dance for the most part, perhaps reflecting the complexity of the steps and the athletic demands that it puts on the dancers. **Natasha and Brendan** also managed to score 27, and in the second series **Jill and Darren** managed the highest Cha Cha Cha score to date, receiving 36 out of 40 in the sixth week of the show. The series three contestants could only manage 32 (**Colin and Zoe**) in comparison.

Quickstep

The Quickstep brings a smile to the face of any ballroom dancer. It's a fast and vibrant dance – not to mention being one of the simpler dances in the ballroom-dancing repertoire!

The fastest and happiest of the ballroom dances takes the couple speeding around the dance floor in a mixture of classic gliding movements and quick kicks and flicks. When it really gets going, the Quickstep can be as dramatic as the Tango, as athletic as the Cha Cha Cha – and it gives the ballroom brigade an opportunity to show off some pretty fancy footwork. Central to the Quickstep technique are the lockstep and the spin turn (see over), but there are also some showy elements of the Charleston and some pure showbiz kicks and drops thrown in there for good measure.

History

As the Foxtrot became the most popular dance of the 20s, bands started to play the music faster and faster, making it hard for all but the most skilful couples to keep up with them. And so the Quickstep was born, incorporating elements of the Charleston – another dance craze that was sweeping America and Europe at the time. English dancers Frank Ford and Molly Spain introduced it into competitions in 1927. Without the large open-leg movements of the Foxtrot, and with several syncopated steps, it soon became even more popular, and evolved into a dynamic dance of seemingly endless possibilities, incorporating hops, runs and rotation.

☻ Tiller Steps

A firm hold in the upper body allows the dancers to show off some fancy footwork made up of kicks and flicks (just like in the Jive). The weight rests lightly on their toes; they're almost floating.

Make-up. Like the Waltz, the women's look is classically glamorous, but here the hair is up. This focuses attention away from the head and on to the dress, which is where all the movement is coming from.

Arms. Back in the classic ballroom hold, the arms will remain in this basic firm position throughout the dance.

Dress. Floating chiffon panels and a layered skirt create a storm of movement around the dancers' legs, resulting in some dramatic effects (see over).

Legs. Rapid shifts of body weight give the Quickstep its skipping, tripping character. And there's far more running than in other ballroom dances.

Feet. Feet are light on the floor throughout the Quickstep, giving an impression of weightlessness. There's no stamping, just quick, light brushes and pivot turns.

Posture. The ballroom hold may be fundamentally the same, but the Quickstep allows the dancers a far greater range of movements. Suppleness is the name of the game.

The Quickstep is all about the mood. It's actually quite a simple dance and there aren't that many steps, so the dancers have to score points by getting the right mixture of smooth, gliding action and fast, showy kicks and flicks. When a Quickstep is done well, you should be watching it with a big grin on your face because it's so light and joyful. Anton and Erin are so light they're almost floating away.

◑ Lockstep

The most basic element of the quickstep. One foot crosses behind the other, allowing the partners to twist and turn their way around the floor.

◑ Lockstep Sequence

The lockstep allows a wide variety of movement. Here Anton goes forward onto his left foot, Erin steps back onto her right and they both cross their feet with the other foot. That's the 'locking' action that gives the step its name.

⦿ Spin Turn

A turning action around each other and the woman brushes her right foot to her left foot, it touches and then comes back again as the man turns her.

➋ Charleston

An element of the 1920s dance craze; here's the characteristic upwards flick of the foot.

➋ Pivots

The dancers place their right feet between each other's legs as they turn continually around each other. The man's tails and the woman's skirt adds size and drama to the movement.

⦿ Hinge Line with Kick

The couple's upper bodies separate like a door from a hinge, and the woman adds the final flourish by kicking her leg up, swinging from her left hip. See how the supporting foot is anchoring the movement under her skirt.

Who Did Well...

Almost everyone, apart from the decidedly earthbound **Diarmuid Gavin**, managed a creditable Quickstep. Natasha and Brendan got the highest marks of the first series (36), but they were pipped by **Denise and Ian** in the series-two final, who were only two points short of Quickstep perfection with 38 out of 40 points. **Colin** raised the bar in the third series with 39.

Samba

It's time to get down and party! This is the ultimate feel-good dance, where hot Latin rhythms and wild, seemingly unrestrained moves give a real flavour of Mardi Gras.

Welcome to Mardi Gras! The Samba is the most explosive and celebratory of all the ten dances, a wild collision of African steps and Brazilian rhythms that's become hugely popular all over the world. Essentially, it's a party dance that's been formalized for competitions, but even under the strict rules of ballroom it retains its unrestrained nature. Sexy costumes, bright colours and up-tempo music make it a favourite with audiences. But be warned: the judges are still looking for technique beneath the sizzling surface!

History

Like the Rumba, the Samba can be traced back to rhythms and steps brought to the New World by African slaves. The name derives from a Bantu word meaning to pray – and the dance and music originated as a way of calling forth the gods and inducing trance in worshippers. The steps were modified during the 19th century, transforming a wide range of steps into a partner dance that began to catch on in the USA and, by the 1920s, in Europe. Further boosts to the Samba's popularity came in the films of Fred Astaire and, in the 1940s, Carmen Miranda. Ballroom Samba, as danced competitively today, was formalized in 1956.

Make-up. The woman should look as if she's ready to go out to the carnival, but the make-up colours are definitely daytime rather than evening. Fake tan is an absolute must if you happen to be naturally pale-skinned like Lilia!

Arms. Where the Samba is concerned, 'straight is great' – not just to achieve the right lines, but in order to allow the dancers to communicate. Here the arms take the line to its ultimate extension.

◐ Rolling Off the Arm

As well as celebrating movement and rhythm, the Samba should also tell a story. Here the woman turns off the man's arm, trying to get away – but he's going to pull her right back.

Dress. Another case of 'less is more'. Women wear cut-away party outfits in bright colours, and there's less movement in the dress, allowing the focus to move to the limbs. If the man's in good shape, out comes the chest.

Feet. Fast and strong through the feet, the Samba demands absolute precision of movement, however extreme. It's important to use the feet as brakes in the fast turns and keep a balanced action throughout.

Legs. The focus tends to be on the straight leg, accentuating the rhythm of the music. The hips and legs should follow complex drum rhythms throughout the dance.

Posture. The woman is on show, but the man is doing all the leading, enabling her to achieve the rolls and freezes that make up many of the sequences. Backs are arched, limbs extended and toned.

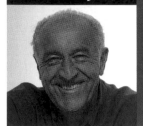

Len Says...

When you watch the Samba you should be transported to Rio de Janeiro for Mardi Gras. Samba music makes everybody want to move their hips, and that's really what it's all about: the looseness and fluidity of the hips and the rhythm that gives to the legs, whether you're travelling or dancing on the spot. A good Samba performance is very sexy. It's not like the seduction of the Rumba; it's much more flirtatious and teasing. The girl's always trying to run away, and he keeps on grabbing her, saying, 'Come here you gorgeous creature!'

◖ Open Rocks

The dancers express the rhythm of the Samba in a series of 'rocks' – strong leg and hip movements – that are executed in a loose (open) hold. Lilia has just flipped her hips across; Darren reflects the line in his position.

● Volta

This is a crossing action of the feet which can be danced either in a straight line (as demonstrated) or in a circle or on the spot.

● Shadow Botafogo

What's a botafogo? It's a move that was invented and popularized at Botafogo Bay in Brazil. The dancer settles on to the straight leg, then goes into a plié on the soft knee. It's called 'shadow' because the two dancers reflect each other's movements.

● Shadow Volta

Just like the volta above, but this time in shadow position, with both dancers facing forward rather than facing each other.

Botafogos Side by Side
The same combination of straight leg and soft knee, but this time the dancers execute the move in the same direction, side by side.

Runs
A travelling step that takes the couple across the floor, then adds an extra element by lifting the knee on the third beat. Another example of Samba storytelling – she's trying to run away, as he tries to keep her.

Shadow Roll
The legs at the back are perfectly parallel at this point, as the dancers move across the floor rotating the body as they go; this is the 'roll' that the judges are looking for.

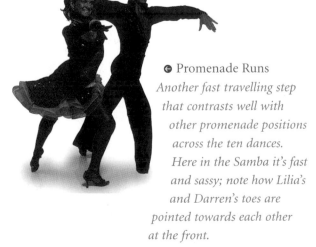

Promenade Runs
Another fast travelling step that contrasts well with other promenade positions across the ten dances. Here in the Samba it's fast and sassy; note how Lilia's and Darren's toes are pointed towards each other at the front.

Who Did Well...

There's been a very wide range of Samba ability on show in *Strictly Come Dancing* – and it's a sure way of telling which of the dancers have got natural rhythm and which haven't. It's particularly hard for the men, who are required to lead the dance and take absolute control. It's greatly to **Aled Jones's** credit that he managed to score 30 out of 40 in the second series, but the best scores overall went to the women: **Natasha** got 37 in series one, **Jill** got 35 in series two, and **Zoe** claimed the Samba crown in series three with an all-time high of 38.

Viennese Waltz

The Viennese Waltz is an elegant, stately dance that is familiar to many. With mercifully few steps, it is simpler than the English Waltz, but still demands a sense of control – and direction!

The 'quick' or Viennese Waltz (as distinguished from the 'slow' or English Waltz) is all based on rotation – the couple simply spins around the floor in 3:4 time. And that, in a nutshell, is that. There are few steps, no jerkiness, no attitudes, just the elegance of continued turns, either travelling or stationary. It's a chance for dancers to show that they're in tune as a couple, that they know how to use the floor and that they can negotiate their way in between other moving dancers without causing a pile-up – which they certainly didn't manage to do in the first series!

History

The faster version of the Waltz (120–180 beats per minute), known as the Viennese, is probably closer in spirit to the dance's peasant origins. Its main antecedent is the Austrian Landler, a dance in triple time, which featured a great deal of hopping and stamping. Moving into the ballrooms of the 19th century, it became faster and more refined, attracting the attention of the great composers of the day including, of course, Johann Strauss. Falling out of favour in the early 20th century, it was revived in the 30s, when it stirred nationalist sentiments during the rise of Nazism, and has remained a dance-floor staple ever since.

Make-up. Once again, elegance and simplicity is key. Erin's hair is up again; with all the turning that this waltz entails, she can't have it flicking in her face all the time.

Arms. The classic ballroom hold remains absolutely, firmly in place throughout the dance. It's vital that the man can steer his partner wherever they need to go, using pressure at the contact points without breaking step.

Dress. As in all the 'smooth' ballroom dances, the skirt is full and flowing to emphasize the grace of the turn, while floating panels exaggerate the movement. Dark colours and sparkling stones give a nocturnal feel.

Feet. The Viennese Waltz is all in the feet. The feet must be absolutely perfect, toned and precise in movement.

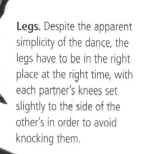

❷ Fleckerl

The classic spin of the Viennese Waltz can be done either way ('natural' or 'reverse') and brings the dancers to their maximum velocity.

Legs. Despite the apparent simplicity of the dance, the legs have to be in the right place at the right time, with each partner's knees set slightly to the side of the other's in order to avoid knocking them.

Posture. Pretty much straight up and down for this dance; it's all about the turns!

Natural Turn

The natural turn is a moving step turning to the right, and on the third step both parties close their feet.

⬇ ⬊ Reverse Turn

The reverse turn is also a travelling step, but on the third step of the reverse turn, the man crosses his left foot in front of his right foot; on the sixth step, the woman crosses her left foot in front of her right foot, and this movement is continued to turn to the left.

Fleckerl

The fleckerl is a stationary turn in which the couple spin on the spot rather than travelling across the floor. Here, Anton and Erin demonstrate both natural and reverse fleckerls.

⊸ Contra Check

In order for the couple to change direction from natural to reverse, they need to start dancing the contra check, in which they suddenly stop moving one way and start going the other.

Salsa

From the clubs of Cuba and Puerto Rico, the Salsa is the least formalized of all the dances. It's all about the rhythm of the music and the movement of the hips – and in the right hands it's hotter than hell.

In its most basic form, the Salsa is the simplest of dances, with a basic step that varies little throughout. But the footwork is only the foundation; from the ankles up, everything has to be rhythmic, swinging and sexy. It's all about the interplay of the couple, moving their bodies together in a way that not only expresses the complex rhythms of Latin music, but which also expresses a sense of attraction, seduction and enjoyment of each other. It's a stationary dance, with compact moves, reflecting its roots in clubs, where there isn't much room for travelling steps. The emphasis is on hip action and spins and, above all, rhythm.

History

Salsa has its roots in Samba, Rumba, mambo and other African and Cuban steps that make up the basic language of Latin dance. The name Salsa means 'sauce' – and it's not just a reference to the dance's sexy nature. It first appeared in the 1940s, in the words of a song by Ignacio Pineiro, with lyrics about eating sausages and a chorus that goes 'Salsaaaaa!'. The term was picked up by DJs in the 50s, who announced songs that 'contained salsa', and gradually came to mean both a style of music (popularized by the great singer Celia Cruz) and a dance style. Now, there are dozens of variations of the salsa, and it remains a highly individualistic dance that can be developed and choreographed to keep it fresh.

◆ Basic Salsa Step

Everything in Salsa is based around a three-step pattern around four beats – in other words, one-two-three-rest. From there onwards, the possibilities are endless. The hold can be closed, or open. The dancers don't travel far, and they remain close and compact, accentuating hip and head movements.

Dress. The woman's dress is all about sex, showing as much flesh as possible. Fringing accentuates the hip movements. Men wear casual jackets and trousers and open-necked shirts to keep the feel loose and informal.

Arms. The free arm should be fluid and rhythmic. The connecting arm should be toned to respond to the partner's lead.

Legs. Salsa has roots in rumba – but where Rumba is all about straightening of the legs, here the emphasis is on keeping the legs flexed and loose.

Feet. The feet are not the focus of the Salsa; they're the engine providing the rhythm while the rest of the body does all the sexy stuff.

Posture. Knees bend and flex, and the dancers stay close and low, giving a feeling of contained energy that burst out through pelvis gyrations.

Make-up. Unlike most Latin dances, in which the hair is put up or back and the make-up tends to be dramatic, dancers favour a more loose, natural look to express Salsa's roots in the clubs. And loose hair accentuates movement.

Len Says...

One of the reasons I love Salsa is because it's the dance that the dance associations never got their hands on. It's kept its naturalness and spontaneity, rather than being formalized to death, like we tend to do with some dances. I first came across it in Miami many years ago. At that time, Miami was full of illegal immigrants from Cuba, and they had the most fantastic clubs in parts of town that you'd never go to alone. Fortunately I had a very good guide who took me into these places, full of young Cubans doing the sexiest dancing I had ever seen. It's basically a Rumba, but very fast – and as it developed it just got hotter and hotter. It remains a club dance, and the emphasis is on rhythm, rhythm, rhythm!

➔ Forward Basic

The beginning of the basic step: the man steps forward, the woman steps back. Here the dancers are in an open hold, just joined at the hands rather than in the more standard hold (see previous page).

➘ Back Basic

The hold has changed – Darren and Lilia are in a closed hold, much closer to a standard ballroom hold – but the step pattern remains the same, as the man steps back and the woman steps forward.

➔ Spin

After the turn, the spin – and, again, this can take many forms. Here, Darren has turned Lilia and then let go of her hands, allowing her to spin freely on her own, coming back, as ever, to the three-step Salsa basic.

➋ ➌ Turning Step

You can do a lot in a Salsa without moving very far across a crowded dance floor. Here's an example of a turn that builds on the basic step, starting with a crossed double-hand hold. The man stays more or less in one place, doing the basic step, while turning the woman 360 degrees around him. She moves under and through his arms, turning fast and spinning on the balls of her feet.

➋ Scoop

Extra drama is added with elaborate steps like this. The woman hooks her left leg over his right, they maintain a strong hold and then he drop her in a scooping semi-circular motion from his left shoulder. Her hair skims the ground and she whips up again on the other side.

➋ ➌ Rocks

The man turns his partner out to right and left, keeping a strong hold and allowing her a full range of hip and head movements. It's in these flourishes that the Salsa really catches fire.

American Smooth

Think classic ballroom dancing, and then loosen things up a bit. The American Smooth gives the dancers more range, more freedom, and more chances to show of their moves.

The American Smooth developed out of standard ballroom dancing as a response to a desire for greater freedom and impact. While ballroom is usually all about maintaining the hold, in American Smooth the dancers can move apart and express themselves through a far greater range of movements. The American Smooth style is found in the Waltz, Foxtrot, Tango and Viennese Waltz. It all starts off with the basic hold, and that's what it comes back to. Smooth transitions mark the change between holds and the 'apart' positions, gliding in and out of sequences with the grace that is always the hallmark of ballroom dancing.

History

In the early 20th century, as ballroom dancing became massively popular all over the world, dance teachers and students became frustrated with the structures of classic ballroom, and developed a style that allowed for greater freedom of expression. In the States, this was popularized by dance studios like Arthur Murray's, and found its fullest expression in the great routines of Fred Astaire and Ginger Rogers. Their free-flowing routines, choreographed by Astaire or Hermes Pan, remain the highwater mark of American Smooth.

Essentially, the American Smooth remains a hybrid of the four dances it comprises – the Waltz, the Tango, the Foxtrot and the Viennese Waltz, combined and revised for maximum 'wow!' factor.

Dress. Think Fred and Ginger – sparkling sophistication for the woman, casual elegance for the man. Stones and accessories add flash and sparkle. The man can wear a tail suit, but more often chooses a lounge or dinner suit.

Arms. The arms should express the music for the Waltz and Foxtrot but they should be flowing, in the Tango they should be sharp and staccato.

Feet. As a general rule the count slow is taken on the heel, and the quick's on the ball of the foot.

◉ Natural Turn

The dancers have just broken out of the ballroom hold and they're setting off into the Viennese Waltz. They step out strongly on the right foot, leading with the heel, before going into a full turn. The essential character of the Viennese Waltz – with its grace and fluidity – is maintained, even though the couple are no longer in a ballroom hold.

Posture. Although the hold is broken for much of the time, the dancers' bodies remain toned throughout. They're erect and elegant; there are none of the low-down, hipshaking moves of Latin dance.

Make-up. In keeping with the free, flowing nature of the dance, Erin's hair and make-up is glamorous but not too dramatic or overstated. The hair is loose but dressed, allowing for movement but dressy enough to set off her outfit.

Legs. Here, they're stepping out into a turn, but elsewhere in the American Smooth they'll run the whole gamut of ballroom lines.

➲ Classic Hold
The couple starts off in classic ballroom hold, feet together, exactly the same as in the ballroom dances. Anton and Erin are demonstrating the Waltz in smooth style. They'll dance for six counts in a standard Waltz box formation – but they're about to break out into the Criss-cross Twinkle step.

➲ Development into Promenade (a V-shaped position with the bodies slightly turned out)
After the underarm passes, the man turns the woman into a promenade position, they resume the ballroom hold and commence forward movement.

⬅ Criss-cross Twinkle
Coming out of the hold, the couple do four underarm passes, changing hands as they move from side to side. It's a variation of a Waltz move, maintaining the essential character of that dance.

◐ ◑ Shadow Grapevine

Here we show a sequence of steps from the Foxtrot, a popular version of the American Smooth. The couple move from side to side, crossing their feet in front and behind three times in the classic grapevine step. There's a rondé at each end of the movement – high on the fourth step, then reversing the move to do a low rondé on the eighth step.

↑ ↗ Natural Turn in Shadow Position

In the Viennese Waltz, breaking out of the ballroom hold, the couple step out on their heels (see previous page) then up on to the toes of the left foot, before progressing through the characteristic Waltz step sequence, turning as they go. The move is completed with the couple coming back to rest with their feet closed.

↘ Lifts

The American Smooth is all about self-expression, and so contestants on Strictly Come Dancing are allowed to put in one lift per routine. There are dozens of variations to be considered; Anton and Erin are demonstrating a side or hitch lift, in which Erin is lifted into the air with her right leg leading the way with effortless ease.

Argentine Tango

Before the Ballroom Tango, there was the Argentine Tango – the original from the bars and clubs of Buenos Aires. It's less formal, much freer, with a looser hold and far more variation.

In Ballroom Tango the hold is set throughout the dance (see pp 150–154), keeping everything tight, angular and rigid. In Argentine Tango, the hold is much freer. It can be very tight, but it can also be loose enough to allow the woman to execute a wide variety of different moves. It can bring the dancers so close they're dancing cheek to cheek, or it can allow a large degree of breathing space between them. Where Ballroom Tango is severe and staccato, Argentine Tango is smooth and soft, the mood is less aggressive and the relationship between the couple more intimate, less confrontational. The enjoyment of the dance comes from the variation in speed from fast pivot turns into slow seductive rocks, combined with clever leg moves, flicks and swivels.

History

From its African roots ('tamgu' means 'to dance' in Niger-Congo languages), the Tango developed in Buenos Aires in the late 19th century. The music that was popular in the bars and clubs of the day fused European, American and African rhythms, and the walking steps that accompanied it form the basis of the tango. Argentine Tango, unlike its later, more formalized ballroom equivalent, has no basic step; instead it is built around a series of improvisations by the couple – these can be anything from a dramatic kneeling pose on the floor to a throwaway oversway. The looseness of Argentine Tango reflects its diverse roots, as new styles and steps came in from all over South America. Without the rules and regulations of its ballroom offshoot, it remains a free, expressive dance.

❂ Argentine Tango Line

The key to the Argentine Tango is passion, demonstrated through a series of 'lines' or positions that the couple dance into. Here you can see how much the Argentine Tango differs from the ballroom version: all semblance of the hold has been abandoned, in favour of a line that expresses intimacy and desire.

Make-up. The whole look of the Argentine Tango is less severe than the ballroom version. The woman's hair is less scraped back, and there's room for some sexy accessories. The make up is less vampy, more sultry.

Arms. The hold can be soft, as here, or hard; variety is the essence of the Argentine Tango. Arms are an expressive tool here, rather than just maintaining the correct ballroom hold.

Feet. In any form of Tango, the feet are doing dozens of jobs; jumping, kicking, dragging, stabbing. Well-toned foot positions extend the lines and add drama to a widely varying series of poses.

Dress. Red and black are the classic colours of the Argentine Tango, again contrasting with the stark monochrome favoured in ballroom. The accents are smart and sexy, with gangster-style ties for the men and high slits on the the women's skirts.

Posture. Variety is the essence here. Unlike the rigid, angular posture of the Ballroom Tango, the Argentine Tango allows the dancers to demonstrate a full range of movements.

Legs. The legs work hard in the Argentine Tango, executing a huge variety of jumps, flicks and hooking kicks. There's always a strong line, focused and tone from the hips right through to the end of the feet, whatever the line.

◔ Argentine Tango Hold

In some ways, this is close to the ballroom hold: however the man's right arm is further around the woman's back, pulling her inwards. But there the similarity ends. It's a much more intimate hold; the heads can be touching, almost cheek-to-cheek, and the man's left hand, together with the lady's right hand, can come right up.

◔ Drop Oversway Line

A highly dramatic line, with the woman's right leg hooked round the man's left thigh. Their other legs shoot out at an angle, and he drops her back into an oversway. This line is a good example of how the arms can straighten in the Argentine Tango; this would never be allowed in the ballroom version.

➔ Rotary Movement

Moving into a typical Argentine Tango line. The woman proceeds to go up on to the balls of her feet and lean dramatically into the man's hold. He then walks around her, turning her on her toes.

➔ Hook and Flick

An example of a small, skilful step that adds variety to the Argentine Tango. The woman's leg darts in between the man's in a series of little hooks and flicks, while the intimate, romantic hold provides contrast in the upper body.

Kneeling Line

This is basically a throwaway oversway that's gone very, very deep, demonstrating the passion of the Argentine Tango through the depth of the line. Again, arms are extended to exaggerate the line.

Profile Line

This line shows just how flexible the hold can be in Argentine Tango. The man's left arm has gone right down to his hip, which you could never do in Ballroom Tango. The leg line is strong and symmetrical, right down to the toes.

Symmetrical Line

This shows clearly some of the differences between the Argentine Tango and the Ballroom Tango: the women's poise, the straight supporting legs and the man's high left arm.

Diagonal Line

No holds are barred in the Argentine Tango; here's a line that emphasises the variation between straightening and flexing of the limbs, and creates a good geometrical shape on the dance floor.

Outside Swivels

The man remains static while the woman does all the work, turning front and back in a series of provocative swivels.

Be Your Own Judge

		Georgina & James	Matt & Lilia	Emma & Darren	Ray & Camilla	Claire & Brendan	Louisa & Vincent	Nicholas & Nicole
Show 1	Your Score							
	Judges' Score							
Show 2	Your Score							
	Judges' Score							
Show 3	Your Score							
	Judges' Score							
Show 4	Your Score							
	Judges' Score							
Show 5	Your Score							
	Judges' Score							
Show 6	Your Score							
	Judges' Score							

Mica & Ian	Ian & Anton	Peter & Erin	Carol & Matthew	Spoony & Alexandra	Mark & Karen	Jimmy & Flavia	Knocked Out

Be Your Own Judge

		Georgina & James	Matt & Lilia	Emma & Darren	Ray & Camila	Claire & Brendan	Louisa & Vincent	Nicholas & Nicole
Show 7	Your Score							
	Judges' Score							
Show 8	Your Score							
	Judges' Score							
Show 9	Your Score							
	Judges' Score							
Show 10	Your Score							
	Judges' Score							
Show 11	Your Score							
	Judges' Score							
The Final	Your Score							
	Judges' Score							

Mica & Ian	Ian & Anton	Peter & Erin	Carol & Matthew	Spoony & Alexsandra	Mark & Karen	Jimmy & Flavia	Knocked Out
							Winner

Next Steps

IMPERIAL SOCIETY OF TEACHERS OF DANCING

The ISTD Dance Examinations Board offers dance examinations in 15 dance genres, including Modern Ballroom and Latin-American. Teachers who offer their examinations can be found throughout the UK and overseas. If you can't find a teacher in your area they will provide a list of schools, just email: education@istd.org.

Imperial House
22–6 Paul Street
London EC2A 4QE

Tel: +44 (0)20 7377 1577
Website: www.istd.org

NATIONAL ASSOCIATION OF TEACHERS OF DANCING

The National Association offers classes and examinations in the following branches: Ballroom, Latin-American, Disco, Street, Rock 'n' Roll, Country & Western Line Dancing, Salsa, Mambo, Merengue, Classical & Modern Sequence. Contact them for more information.

NATD
44–7 The Broadway
Thatcham
Berkshire RG19 3HP

Tel: + 44 (0) 1635 868888
Website: www.natd.org.uk

INTERNATIONAL
DANCE TEACHERS' ASSOCIATION

Log on to their website to find a dance teacher or course near you – all over the world – or contact them direct and they will send you a free and comprehensive list of IDTA-registered teachers in your area.

**International House
76 Bennett Road
Brighton
East Sussex BN2 5JL**

**Tel: +44 (0)1273 685652
Website: www.idta.co.uk**

UNITED KINGDOM ALLIANCE OF PROFESSIONAL
TEACHERS OF DANCING

Log on to their website or contact the UKA direct for guidance on finding your nearest registered dance teacher.

**Centenary House
38–40 Station Road
Blackpool
FY4 1EU**

**Tel: +44 (0)1253 408828
Website: www.ukadance.co.uk**